Successful Marketing for Small Businesses

Nigel Hill

Letts

First published 1990
by Charles Letts & Co Ltd
Diary House, Borough Road, London SE1 1DW

Illustrations: Kevin Jones Associates
© Charles Letts & Co Ltd

British Library Cataloguing in Publication Data
Hill, Nigel
  Successful marketing for small businesses
  1. Great Britain. Marketing for small firms
  I. Title
  658.8

ISBN 0–85097–881–5

The Author

Nigel Hill BSc (Econ), MPhil, DipM, MCIM is Marketing Director of JPD
Associates Ltd, a company with interests in management consultancy, training
and manufacturing. He has published numerous articles and two textbooks on
marketing, and is author of the companion volume *Starting a Small Business.*
Nigel has previously worked in management positions in the manufacturing,
retailing and service sectors, largely with small companies. In his current role
he provides marketing, business planning and training support to JPD's clients.
He has assisted in the starting up of many small firms and businesses.

Readers please note: Some of the information in this book, particularly that which is
directly influenced by government policy, and the contact addresses and telephone
numbers of useful organizations, is liable to change. From May 1990 the London
telephone code *01* will be replaced by *071* or *081.*
  It should also be noted that, where words have been used which denote the masculine
gender only, they shall be deemed to include the feminine gender, and vice versa.

Printed and bound in Great Britain by
Charles Letts (Scotland) Ltd

Foreword

Beating the competition

One thing which we as bankers share with our customers is the need to succeed in the face of intense and changing competition.

In our experience, all products and services have to confront that challenge. Even if you believe that you have come up with the entrepreneur's jackpot, the idea that everyone needs but no one else can offer, we can assure you that, by the time it has been converted into reality, the competitors will be assembling!

This book looks at successful marketing as the essential companion of competition, the link between the small business and the marketplace.

Bob Maiden
Managing Director
The Royal Bank of Scotland

Contents

1 The importance of marketing

Aims of this chapter

Marketing is about building a successful business through **winning and keeping customers**. This chapter will develop the ideas on which the marketing philosophy is based, including:

- The difference between the production, sales and marketing concepts
- Inward and outward looking companies
- The importance of customer service
- The role that marketing can play for your firm

The following case study provides an interesting and informative view of the importance of marketing for the small business.

Seamus Connolly: an engineer who believes in marketing

Seamus Connolly's route to starting his own business was typical of many new business start-ups. He was an engineer who saw a way of improving on an existing product: he developed a simple, lightweight, easily assembled container for storing liquids and granular materials. Potentially it had a very wide range of applications. For example, a relief organization, such as OXFAM, could use it to store and transport food supplies for a third world disaster area. Alternatively, a chemical processing company could use it for the storage of raw materials, or a laboratory for the storage of samples. The product was innovative, it offered users so much more than existing, broadly similar products and it had so many potential applications, that, thought Seamus, it was bound to sell.

So far, Seamus's route into business was typical. He had a very good, technically sound product idea which had arisen out of his own personal experience and expertise. At this point, however, his progress towards self-employment began to deviate from the norm. Many people take it for granted that their product is bound to sell (because it is so good), and they literally rush into production.

Seamus did not do this. Partly because his product was so innovative, his start-up costs would be high. In a bid to raise the necessary capital he entered a small business competition sponsored by the Bank of Ireland which offered a substantial cash prize for the winner. Preparing the submission for the competition involved the compilation of a large amount of marketing information in order to produce a business plan explaining who would buy the product, why they would buy it and how the company would draw their attention to the product and its benefits. Seamus had to develop a marketing strategy involving sales projections to different market segments such as military organizations, chemical companies, relief organizations and so on.

Without the demands of the competition, Seamus believes that he would have spent more time focusing on the requirements of getting his new business started, such as product development and raising finance. He thinks he would probably have started his business sooner, but he also believes that its chances of success would have been greatly reduced. Spending time developing his marketing plan forced Seamus to speak to potential customers and find out exactly what their requirements were, how often they purchased such a product and what they thought of his own product idea. It forced him to really get to know the competition, to study their products and their promotional literature and to figure out how he could get his message across to potential buyers in a better way.

In carrying out his market research Seamus made some very useful contacts. For example, he met field personnel of a disaster relief organization in London who told him about the problems they were having with emergency supplies. They complained of nuts and bolts falling off the equipment and getting lost and of a shortage of maintenance skills and tools on site in many third world countries. As a result of such information Seamus was able to design a product which was simple to assemble and did not require nuts, bolts, spanners or skilled men. He was thus able to offer customers a product which made a real contribution to solving their problems and making their life easier.

Seamus Connolly won the competition and the cash prize helped him to launch Fast Engineering Ltd and his innovative product 'Fastank'. Success followed, with the company showing strong growth. Seamus attributes his success to grafting the marketing philosophy onto the technical skills he already possessed.

Entering the competition forced Seamus to focus his attention outwards on customers rather than inwards on his own product and his own internal requirements. It enabled him to develop a customer oriented philosophy from the outset. This attitude has since guided the development of his business. Whether working on a new product, reading a trade journal or preparing a brochure, Seamus finds his mind focuses on the question of how the activity will help his company to offer more satisfaction to customers. Every small business owner should do the same.

Three business philosophies

It is the main objective of all firms to make profits but views about how to run the business to maximize these profits differ. As far as small companies are concerned this 'business philosophy' is often influenced by the vocational background and temperament of the owner. For example, an engineer or a craftsman will be naturally inclined to place emphasis on product quality. There are three business philosophies which strongly influence the running of companies, subconsciously directing all decisions and priorities. They are: the *production* concept, the *sales* concept, and the *marketing* concept.

The production concept

According to the production concept the key to business success is to be better at 'producing' than your competitors. This outlook is perfectly described by a much quoted comment made by the American Ralph Waldo Emerson in the 19th century:

'If a man build a better mousetrap, even though he live in a wood, the world will beat a path to his door'.

It is assumed that a better product, a more advanced gadget, a product with more features, is the way to competitive advantage in the marketplace. However, as the case study below demonstrates, this philosophy does not always work, even when all logic seems to dictate that an innovative new product will succeed. In the marketplace, success may be determined by customers' fickle preferences, illogical choices or in their conservative belief in traditional methods.

The plasterers' friend

Steve Jodrell was working as a plasterer. His problem lay in the method of mixing the plaster, which had remained unchanged for centuries. Most plaster is gypsum based and is supplied in the form of a very low density brown powder which has to be mixed with water. Traditionally this is done on site by plasterers in a large container, usually an old tin bath. It is backbreaking and time consuming work. It can take nearly as long to mix the plaster as it does to apply it to the walls. There must, thought Steve, be a better way. He didn't see bricklayers mixing cement by hand with a shovel.

Being technically minded, Steve set to work in his spare time to invent the plasterer's equivalent of a cement mixer. It was a technically demanding task because the mix consistency of plaster is critical and needs to be varied to meet differing conditions. The development of the machine took several years and a lot of money. It outstripped Steve's resources, but he found a backer and continued the development on a full-time basis. Eventually, following an investment of some tens of thousands of pounds, the product, named the 'Joddymix', was perfected and patented.

The Joddymix was the answer to plasterers' prayers. All they had to do was to tip a full bag of plaster into the machine's storage container, place its hose in a reservoir of water, set the mixture dial and turn it on. The machine then produced a perfect plaster mix, consistently better in quality than was normally achieved by hand mixing. The benefits were obvious. No more backbreaking mixing; increased productivity, since skilled plasterers could now spend all their time plastering rather than mixing, and a cleaner, healthier working environment. Moreover, as a result of the improved productivity, the capital cost of the machine could be recovered in about three months. The patented machine had no competitors and, following a letter to the BBC, it was featured on the *Tomorrow's World* programme. In theory, the product could not fail.

However, markets do not always behave in a predictable way and the owners of Joddymix Ltd were in for a severe shock. In order to make production as efficient as possible, they had decided to manufacture the machine in batches of 25, and did not envisage too much difficulty finding homes for the first batch. And yet, three years after the machine appeared on *Tomorrow's World*, the company still hadn't sold all of these first 25 machines.

This illustrates the danger of taking it for granted that a good new product is bound to sell.

The production concept can also lead to an obsession with internal efficiency. Some people believe that the key to business success is to be an efficient producer, enabling the company to cut its costs and therefore sell at a lower price. However, this is not always the case.

Henry Ford: over efficient?

Henry Ford, the car manufacturer, pioneered mass production but then became carried away with the objective of ever greater economies of scale. Everything in the company was built around the need for production efficiency culminating in their famous 1920s slogan: 'You can have any colour you like as long as it's black'. Yes, it was more efficient to produce only black cars and yes, as a result of this philosophy Ford did sell the cheapest cars on the market. However, Alfred Sloan, at General Motors, believed that customers wanted more choice. He offered red cars, blue ones and other colours. He added unnecessary luxury items inside the car which all added to the cost. Although General Motors could not match Ford's low prices, their sales and market share grew, even during the depression years of the 1930s. Before the Second World War, they had overtaken Ford and have never since lost their position as the world's largest manufacturer of cars.

Of course it is important to have a good product. Of course it is important to innovate and develop new products. Of course it is important to be an efficient producer. All of these things will help your small business to succeed, but, in themselves, they will not guarantee success. Increasing competition has made it unwise to rely on 'the world beating a path to your door', however much better your new 'mousetrap' may be. You need to go out and sell it – hence the development of the sales concept.

The sales concept

According to the sales concept the key to success in business is the ability to sell hard and effectively. In all markets, persuasion in its broadest sense, whether through personal contact, advertising, catalogues or some other method of communication, is almost always necessary if sales are to be made in any volume. The chief mistake of the owners of Joddymix was to assume that the product would more or less sell itself. They had not realized the extent to which the techniques of persuasion were necessary to sell even a very good product.

The marketing concept

However, as the 20th century progresses, the techniques of persuasion are less able to guarantee success than they were some decades ago. Trends towards more equal societies, universal education, and improvements in communications have all contributed to more knowledgeable and discriminating buyers. Customers are more demanding, more confident and more aware of their rights. Their expectations concerning factors like quality and customer service are increasing all the time. So, in the 1990s the marketing concept is more relevant than the sales concept.

Winning and keeping customers. According to the marketing concept the main objective of all firms should be the winning and keeping of satisfied customers. It follows that all activity within the company should be directed towards satisfying the needs of customers. The marketing concept suggests that those businesses which put into practice the philosophy of 'putting the customer first' at all times will have the most success in the marketplace, because customers will gravitate towards those companies which offer them the most satisfaction, the best deal, and the best value for money. As shown below, this can be done even before the business is off the ground!

Marketing in action

A famous marketing story tells of a man who walked into an advertising agency in New York in the early years of this century.

'I want the world's best ever shampoo advert,' said the man, 'can you do that?'

'Of course!' replied the modest advertising man.

'Good. Let me know when you've done it,' said the marketeer, turning on his heels and beginning to leave the room.

'Hold on,' shouted the astonished adman, 'what about the product? What's it like? What colour is it? What's it called? What does the packaging look like?'

'Oh, I'm leaving all that to you,' replied the shampoo man, as he left.

The advertising guru was obviously perplexed. This was not the normal way of going about things! How could he make an advert with no product to sell?

After a long hard think, he decided that if he had no shampoo to sell, he had better go out and ask people what shampoo they wanted to buy. He sent his staff out onto the New York streets, asking lots of people lots of questions. They asked questions about how people washed their hair, which shampoo they used, what the good and bad points about their shampoo were, what kind of packaging they liked, whether colour mattered, where they usually bought it and what was a fair price.

Amazingly, the agency found that as a result of all these questions they were able to draw up an identikit picture of the kind of shampoo which would most please a good proportion of shampoo buyers. They had information about the style of packaging, colour, aroma, strength, price and the kind of outlets from which customers would prefer to buy the product. From this information they could mock-up visuals showing the product and write copy describing the product.

Having produced the ad, the agency invited back the shampoo man. 'Here it is,' said the agent, 'what do you think?'

'Great. Just the kind of thing I was looking for.'

'Pleased we could be of service.' Still somewhat confused however, the adman continued: 'but how can this advert be sufficiently close to your product to be of any value to you?'

'Easy', said the shampoo man. 'It is my product.' He proceeded to explain that rather than develop a product on the basis of his own personal views, he was going to base it on the product in the advert.

The man went away and organized the manufacture of the product to the specification described in the advert. He priced it according to the agent's information and sold it through appropriate outlets.

The man's name was Alberto Culver. His business succeeded.

Inward and outward looking companies

The three business concepts can be summarized into the two broad categories of inward and outward looking companies.

Inward looking companies

An inward looking company is likely to think like this:

'The purpose of selling is to ensure that the customer buys the product (or service) that we supply'.

Inward looking companies will follow a product or sales oriented philosophy (or both). They will tend to plan and organize their business and develop new products according to their own subjective opinion of what represents a good idea or a product which will sell.

The thought processes of the inward looking businessman might go something like this:

1 This new electric corkscrew would be a good idea.
2 Let's make some.
3 Let's make 1000.
4 Let's charge £10 each.
5 Now let's get out there and sell them!

If the entrepreneur is right, and his own views on the value of electric corkscrews are held by many other people, he will probably make a lot of money. But what if he is mistaken? What if consumers see electric corkscrews as a ridiculous gimmick and shops refuse to stock them because they do not envisage any demand for the product? The inward looking entrepreneur who takes 'seat of the pants' decisions can never be sure that there will be a demand for his products. He acts out of belief and self-confidence. There are many spectacular success stories of businessmen whose companies were based on entrepreneurial beginnings, such as Richard Branson and Alan Sugar, but there are many more failures whose stories are rarely brought to public attention.

Outward looking companies

An outward looking company is more likely to believe in the following statement:

'The purpose of marketing is to provide the product (or service) that the customer wants to buy'.

It is a matter of common sense that the business which supplies exactly the kind of product which the customer wishes to buy is greatly increasing its chances of success. Therefore, like Alberto Culver, the outward looking company will devote considerable time and effort to researching and identifying customers' needs.

The thought processes of the outward looking businessman might go something like this:

1 Let's see if people have any problems opening bottles.
2 Let's see if we can develop a product to solve those problems.
3 Let's see if people like our solution.
4 Let's find out how much they will pay for it.

5 Let's decide if it's profitable.
6 Now let's make some!

As anybody who has ever tried to sell anything well knows, selling a product which people want to buy is an easy, enjoyable and very satisfying activity. Trying to sell a product which people are not particularly keen on buying is a very difficult, unpleasant and frustrating activity.

Customers

Put yourself in the customer's shoes

The best way to make yourself outward looking is to put yourself in the customer's shoes. As individuals, and, maybe as business buyers, we are all customers. We all know what it feels like to receive good service and, sometimes, to be the victims of appalling service. The company which goes out of its way to give good service will almost always receive the same custom again. Moreover, the satisfied customer will act as an ambassador for the business, singing its praises to friends and colleagues. However, the disgruntled customer will also broadcast his views, alienating, in the process, unknown numbers of potential buyers.

The recovery of Jaguar

According to Sir John Egan, the chairman of Jaguar cars: 'business is about making money from satisfied customers. Without satisfied customers there can be no future for any commercial organization'.

To rescue Jaguar from the brink of bankruptcy, Egan initiated a survey of all recent Jaguar buyers to obtain their views on the car they had purchased. The level of customer dissatisfaction was alarming, but its causes were usually a series of trivial faults, such as rattles, rust spots, the failure of components supplied by sub-contractors and the poor availability of spare parts, rather than any problems caused by major engineering or design weaknesses. Customers still considered Jaguars to be fine cars but felt that they were so shoddily put together, and the after sales service was so poor, that Jaguar could not be a company that cared about its customers; which was why it was losing so many. Egan determined to put this right. He didn't need to introduce new models or to make sweeping changes in the existing product. He concentrated initially on introducing a series of small measures which would simply demonstrate that Jaguar was a company which did care about its customers. New quality assurance procedures were developed to ensure that Jaguars were properly assembled. Similar quality standards were imposed on suppliers of components. These measures eliminated the vast majority of niggling little faults which had so alienated Jaguar customers during the 1970s. Egan also ensured that adequate supplies of spare parts were made available to dealers and the company contacted all customers a few weeks after the purchase of their new Jaguar to ensure that they were happy with their new car or to solve any problems they may be having before those problems escalated into a major cause of customer dissatisfaction. Through the introduction of such simple, common sense measures, Jaguar soon began to recover its reputation as a producer of fine cars.

Egan transformed Jaguar from an inward looking organization to an outward looking company whose chief objective was to satisfy its customers. Although Jaguar is a large company this case study is important because the simple marketing philosophy it illustrates equally applies to all small businesses.

Focus on customers

It is often said that marketing is about markets, market research, assessing market demand, and so on. It is not. It is about customers, understanding customers' requirements and behaviour and giving those customers exactly the kind of product or service they want. It is, therefore, essential to focus at the customer level rather than at the market level.

1 **Knowing your customers.** Marketing success is usually based on a deep understanding of customers and on close relationships with them. In this respect, small businesses often have a significant advantage over their larger competitors because the decision makers in a small firm are naturally close to their customers, often through regular pesonal contact. Large companies often have to carry out extensive market research in order to try to achieve an adequate level of understanding of their customers. You should never underestimate this natural advantage. As you grow, resist all pressures to become more remote from your customers.

2 **Putting customers first.** Sometimes, putting customers first will be inconvenient and may be inefficient, but you must do it. Customers always know if you are not putting them first.

The role of marketing

Bridging the gap

Many people see the chief role of marketing as building a bridge between the firm and its customers.

The purpose of building the bridge is to bring the whole firm, including everyone who works for it, closer to its customers. The closer it is, the more likely it is to understand their requirements, to meet those needs in a satisfactory way and to communicate a caring attitude towards its customers.

Who is responsible for marketing?

Although the small business must strive for closeness with its customers, it is a mistake to view this objective as a task which can be delegated. It is hardly likely that one individual, such as a salesman, or one department, called 'Marketing', will successfully make the firm customer orientated. Responsibility for the satisfaction of customers' needs must lie with everyone in the company. For example, the workers on the shop floor have a huge impact through their ability to produce a high quality product on time. The office staff may reduce customers' satisfaction if they are slow in processing the orders, inaccurate in the provision of documentation or discourteous in the collection of payment. Delivery drivers, receptionists, installation or service engineers as well as the sales staff and senior management – all can have a significant effect on customer satisfaction.

There is mounting evidence that a good reputation for customer service is crucial to all firms' ability to compete successfully in the marketplace.

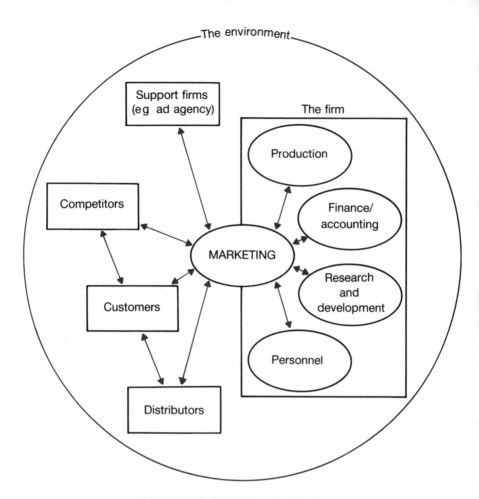

Fig. 1.1 The bridge building role of marketing

More and more companies are devoting time and resources to making sure that all their staff understand the importance of customers and behave in the 'right' way towards them. Customers know which firms are genuinely helpful and tend to gravitate towards them. Following this simple principle of treating your customers well is much more important to the long-term success of your small business than any sophisticated advertising or selling technique. It is a theme which will be discussed further in Chapters 8 and 9.

Summary

1 Products and businesses start with customers' needs. The basis on which all new business should be formed is not just a new product idea, (however good or innovative it appears to be), but a clear need expressed

by customers which could be met by your new product idea or an obvious problem which the product could help customers to overcome.

2 Products still need to be made and sold well. Although it is generally recognized that neither the production nor the sales concept is, in itself, sufficient to ensure success in business, these ideas are important pieces in the jigsaw of company performance. To be competitive a firm must manufacture its product or provide its service efficiently. Also, however good its product, any business must be prepared to sell it hard and employ all the powers of persuasion that are open to it.

3 Firms and their employees must be outward looking. The best way of ensuring that your company consistently meets the needs of its customers is to adopt an outward looking philosophy. This means being able to put yourself in your customers' shoes, adopt a true customer focus and see things from their point of view.

4 Competitive advantage comes from satisfying customers. The best way to beat the competition is to fully embrace the marketing philosophy: offer your customers the best all-round service.

5 Marketing is a three step process. The role of marketing is to help the business to adopt a true customer focus. This can be broken down into three steps:
a the company must understand its potential customers, their needs and their priorities
b it must develop a product or service which meets those customer needs more effectively than its competitors
c it must inform potential customers that the product or service exists and demonstrate how it does meet their needs better than competing products or services

Action

1 What are the key factors (excluding price) which give customers an incentive to opt for your company rather than one of your competitors?

2 How good is your customer service? Why not approach (by letter or telephone) your own company in the guise of a potential customer to see how well your staff respond to customer enquiries or how friendly and helpful they would appear to an outsider?

2 Selecting the right market

Aims of this chapter

If you are going to satisfy your customers' needs you have to start by selling a product or service that people want to buy. Selling the right thing at the right time to the right people is vital to your business success. Gathering information to make sure that you enter the right markets with a suitable product or service, aimed at people who want to buy them, is rather like moving down a funnel (see fig. 2.1).

The next few chapters will take you down this funnel. This chapter will examine:

● The general trends that can affect the fortunes of all businesses

● The way to analyse the attractiveness of specific markets

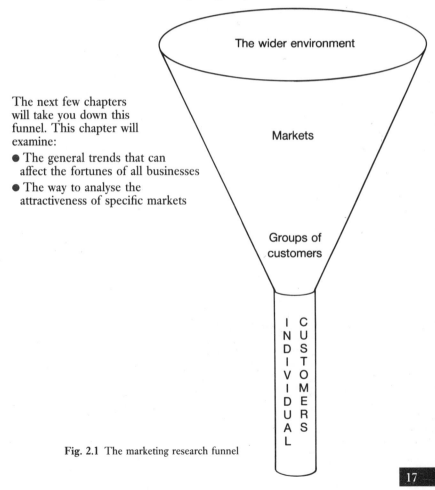

Fig. 2.1 The marketing research funnel

The 'pest' factors

In trying to select attractive markets for your firm, the starting point is the scanning of trends in the marketplace. Your objective is to identify trends which should offer good marketing opportunities which your company would be in a strong position to exploit. Unfortunately not all trends will be favourable: some will be threats to your company rather than opportunities. It is equally important to be alive to the threats so that your company's path can be steered away from them.

You need to be well informed about trends in the following four broad environments:

a political environment
b economic environment
c social environment
d technological environment

Political trends

New legislation offers opportunities to some companies and threats to others. For example, new laws tightening up on drink-driving would be beneficial to companies offering soft or low alcohol drinks, but would threaten the sales of any companies that were entrenched in the alcoholic drinks sector. The more alert companies are to pending legislation the more thoroughly they can prepare themselves to exploit opportunities or to avoid potential threats.

Signs and Labels Ltd: new laws mean business

Signs and Labels Ltd is a Stockport based firm which was formed in 1970 and has specialized in industrial safety signs and associated items. Throughout the 1970s the government was placing more emphasis on health and safety in industry. Regulations were introduced which required companies to be much more thorough in using signs and labels to signal potential dangers in areas such as offshore installations, gas safety, the handling of hazardous materials and so on. This culminated in the Safety Signs Regulations of 1980 which led to a huge growth in the company's market.

Political trends do not always manifest themselves in the form of legislation. For instance, the market for safety signs was growing even before they became compulsory (though its growth really took off after the passing of the legislation). The current growing unacceptability of drink-driving is bound to affect the drinks industry whether or not new legislation reaches the statute book. You must therefore be alert to the implications of political trends that are influenced by pressure groups. The current preoccupation in the UK, and the Western world, with ecological issues and 'environment friendly' products is an excellent example of how trends can have a major impact on the marketplace.

The Body Shop

In the mid 1970s, the first Body Shop opened in a side street in Brighton, financed by a £4000 bank loan. Anita Roddick, the founder of the shop, wanted to sell pure cosmetic and toiletry products which involved no cruelty to animals at any stage of the production chain. Horrified by the fact that in the cosmetics industry the packaging could account for up to 85 per cent of production costs, she wanted to sell her products without promotional hype such as unnecessary packaging or expensive adverts in glossy magazines. She was sure that many people shared her views. They obviously did, and as the green revolution gathered momentum in the 1980s, so did the expansion of The Body Shop. By 1988 the company had 111 outlets in the UK and many more overseas. By the end of June 1989 Anita Roddick's shares in the company had a stockmarket value of £46 million, making her the 26th wealthiest business person in the UK.

1 Political trends affect all businesses. For example, the green revolution is already affecting a significant proportion of businesses operating in the UK. The food industry, the plastics and packaging industries, the timber trade, and businesses dealing in cosmetics, leathers, furs and paper have all come under the green microscope.

2 Swim with the tide. It should be clear that swimming with the tide of political trends and legislation is generally much more sensible than ignoring or going against such trends. You must always try to identify a path that leads to growth markets rather than static or declining markets. Political trends and pending legislation often signpost those paths.

3 Sources of information. Information about political trends is all around us, on television, in the newspapers and in conversations with friends and colleagues. As a small businessman your task is to constantly interpret political events in terms of their meaning for your firm. For example, headline news about the discovery of fragments of glass in jars of baby food should ring opportunity bells for a packaging firm specializing in shrink wrap sleeving.

However, in order to become and remain well informed you need to be systematic. You should:

1 Read your own trade magazines very carefully. Check in *Benn's Media Directory* (see Chapter 10) that you are aware of all relevant journals.

2 Join a trade association and go to its meetings. Good trade associations keep their members informed of important developments and you can learn a lot from talking to fellow members. The *Directory of British Associations* gives details of all trade bodies.

3 Consult indexes or cuttings from newspaper and magazine articles such as the *Clover Newspaper Index* or *McCarthy* 'cards'. They are indexed, helping you to locate relevant information.

4 Her Majesty's Stationery Office (HMSO) publish details of all forthcoming legislation in the form of Green Papers (still under discussion) and White Papers (pending legislation).

5 Growing integration with the European Community means that much of Britain's future legislation will be prompted by European directives. Details can be obtained from the European Commission office in London.

The Department of Trade and Industry offer a hotline on the Single European Market: *01 200 1992*. They also produce some booklets on new European directives and standards and a regular newspaper called *Single Market News*, which is available free of charge.

Full details of all reference sources are included in Chapter 5. In reality you will consult most in a public library rather than buy them so Chapter 5 also gives details of the main business libraries in the UK.

Economic trends

Unemployment, interest rates, the value of the pound, inflation, the growth in National Income! Many small businesses do not see the relevance to their own marketing of the national economic trends and statistics which bombard us every day in the press and on the news, but the business owner soon sees their relevance to himself if, for example, interest rates go up and he has a large overdraft or a large personal mortgage. Remember that all these trends may similarly affect a company's customers and therefore need to be taken into account in its marketing planning.

1 **Isolate the relevant economic trends.** Some of these economic trends will affect your company more than others. The British economy may be growing at the rate of 3 per cent per annum, but some business sectors will be booming, others declining. Tracking all economic trends would be both time-consuming and unnecessary. Your main task is to isolate the economic indicators which have the most important effect on your own business. As shown below, it may be the effect of economic trends on your customers or your customer's customers which eventually hit your own business.

Interest rates and the building market

High interest rates mean expensive mortgages which tend to deter people from buying new houses unless they have to move with their work. It happened during the inflationary period of the late 1970s, with the house building market declining at about 2 per cent per annum between 1975 and 1982. In stark contrast the market growth was 8 per cent per annum between 1986 and 1988, before the imposition of high interest rates again led to decline. A builder of new houses can draw useful conclusions from these past figures to help with his own planning. But what about suppliers to the building industry, further back in the chain of demand. How will it affect them?

Close scanning of the environment helped one small timber merchant to change course to minimize the threat posed by higher interest rates. Regular scanning of the trade press helped the company to spot a special report on trends in the building trade, prepared by industry analysts, SBC Stockbroking. The report brought home the real threat of high mortgage rates, predicting a fall in demand of 20 per cent for new housing by 1991. The resulting overcapacity in the industry would cause problems for many companies.

However, the report did identify some opportunities in the industry. As shown in the bar chart opposite, some sectors of the industry were more attractive than others, particularly the repair, maintenance and improvements sector (RMI) which has been taking a growing share of building industry expenditure. Forecasts from the National Council of

Building Material Producers predicted that the RMI sector would continue to grow at a rate in excess of 3 per cent per annum. If people could not afford to buy new houses, they were more likely to improve their existing one.

The message was clear. Companies involved in the building trade which would best avoid the consequences of higher interest rates would be those with the least involvement in new house building and the greatest involvement in RMI. Thus, in targeting his selling and promotional effort the timber merchant was able to give less emphasis to house builders and devote more effort to those companies heavily involved in RMI.

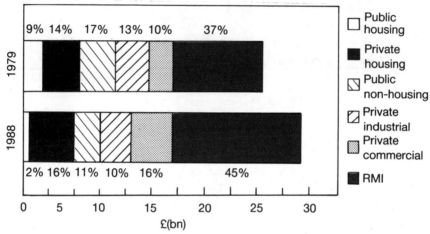

Fig. 2.2 Identifying economic trends: the building industry

2 Sources of information. The example above shows the value of trade journals as a source of information and Chapter 5 gives many sources of economic statistics. In particular the *Annual Abstract of Statistics* is a good brief guide. If you sell in consumer markets the *Marketing Pocketbook* is a good guide to economic and social trends.

Social trends

Ultimately, all demand in the marketplace derives from the spending power of people. Firms selling directly to consumer markets will be quickly affected by social trends such as population growth, changes in the demographic profile (see fig. 2.4), changes in lifestyles and changes in fashions. Companies operating in business to business markets will ultimately be affected by the same trends.

1 Demographic trends affecting business. As can be seen from the graph overleaf, the number of people in the youth market is declining sharply. In fact, there will be around two million fewer 15 to 24 year olds in the UK in 1995 compared with 1985, representing a decline of over 20 per cent. Firms which rely on this age group for a significant proportion of their business (discotheques, fashion shops, sports goods manufacturers) can expect to feel the consequences of this demographic trend.

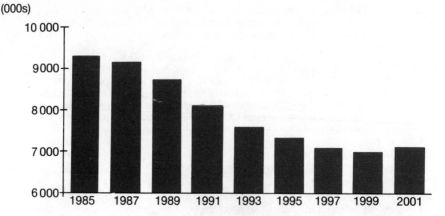

(000s)

Fig. 2.3 The population of 15 to 24 year olds
Source: *Government Actuary*

On the other hand, some age groups are growing. The 'starter family' age group of 25 to 34 year olds will increase by 1.3 million people, or 17 per cent, over the same period. As far as most businesses are concerned, the most critical implications involve the effect of these demographic trends on the total spending power of different age groups. Fig. 2.4 shows that markets involving heavy concentrations of 25 to 34 year olds or 45 to 59 year olds are showing the strongest growth.

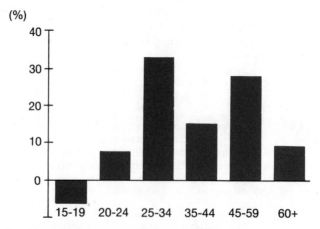

(%)

Fig. 2.4 Percentage change (1987–93) in the spending power of different age groups
Source: *Henley Centre*

Of course, the expenditure of different age groups is influenced by many factors, including their earnings potential, inheritance and the extent of their family commitments as well as the total number of individuals within that age group. Taking all such factors into consideration, the

Henley Centre has predicted strong growth markets for family and baby products, DIY and other home based activities, baby and child care services and family-oriented financial services.

The 45 to 59 year old age group looks particularly interesting for marketers. Due to other social trends such as early retirement and the spread of owner occupancy (this group will be the first one to really benefit through inheriting their parents' homes), the 45 to 59 year olds will be a very affluent market segment with high levels of discretionary spending power. They will be financially independent, healthy and active, which should be good news for markets such as holidays, tourist attractions, restaurants, gardening products, home furnishings and appropriately targeted fashion stores.

Many other social trends such as the growth in the number of single parents, the increasing number of working mothers, and the growing number of elderly people, can offer opportunities to the alert small businessman. Directing your company's path towards favourable social trends is clearly the objective.

2 **Sources of information.** The government produces many reports on social trends, such as *Social Trends, Regional Trends, Household Survey* and *Family Expenditure Survey*, all of which are available from HMSO and major libraries.

Technological trends

The pace of technological change is constantly accelerating, posing real threats for those businesses which do not keep fully abreast of the latest developments but offering attractive opportunities for those close to 'the state of the art'. The implications of technological change are no longer confined to 'high-tech' sectors such as electronics. Virtually all walks of business life are being affected by the information technology revolution. Retailers are using bar codings and Epos (Electronic point of sale) systems to increase their competitiveness, and we may soon be witnessing the widespread adoption of Eftpos (Electronic funds transfer at point of sale) by retailers to switch money directly from customers' bank accounts to their own as the purchase is made. Innovations such as desk top publishing have revolutionized the medium of the printed word. All these developments can be profitably exploited by the small business.

Sources of information. Your own trade journals and associations almost certainly present you with the best opportunity for keeping up with relevant technological developments. Exhibitions are very good places to catch up with new developments. The *Exhibition Bulletin* provides a comprehensive, well indexed listing of all exhibitions in the UK. There are also some useful compilations such as *Current Technology Index* and *Finding and Using Product Information* (details in Chapter 5).

Markets for products and services

It is now time to advance further down the marketing research funnel. Regular scanning of trends in the environment will help to identify general areas of opportunity and threat facing the firm. You now need to begin the process of zooming in on more precise opportunities for specific products or services in identifiable markets.

Your objective at this stage is to paint a clear picture of a specific market which represents an opportunity for a product or service which your firm could supply. You can then use this information to evaluate the potential attractiveness of the opportunity. This section will outline the kind of details which you should know about a proposed new market. Chapter 5 will explore research methods which can be used to acquire the information.

Market size

If you need to spend large sums of money on machinery, buildings, research and development, stock, advertising or on any other investment in order to enter a proposed new market, you need to be sure that the market is large enough to offer the prospect of a return on that investment. The larger your investment relative to your estimate of the market size, the more important it is to obtain accurate figures of market size.

Market size will often be important for firms operating in very specialized markets. However, many small firms have turnovers which are

If you are a big fish in a small pond

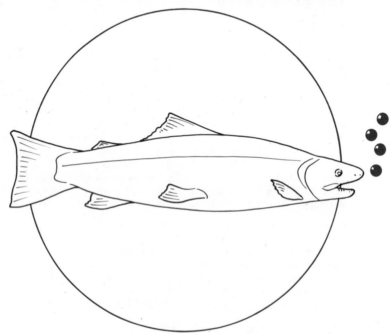

your well-being may depend on the pond
being large enough

Fig. 2.5 For some firms market size is important

tiny in relation to the size of the market in which they operate. If you are in that position, the considerable time and expense which may be involved in ascertaining accurate market size figures would be better utilized on other aspects of market research such as analysing the competition or getting to know the needs and priorities of individual customers.

If you are a small fish in a big pond

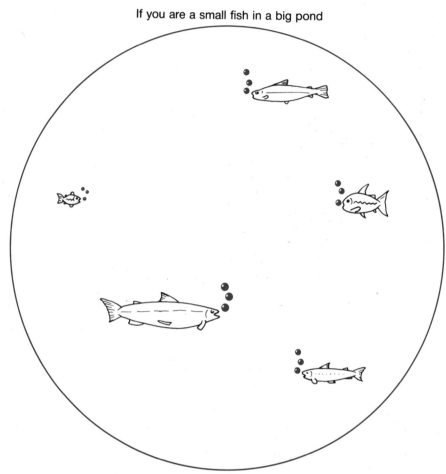

it is not the size of the pond which will
determine your survival

Fig. 2.6 For some firms market size is unimportant

Market growth

The best opportunities usually arise from areas of growth. If the 'pond' is getting bigger there will be room for new fish to enter without preventing the growth of the existing fish. In such circumstances the big fish will not

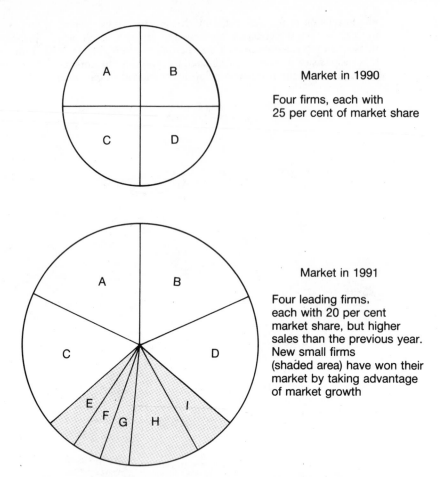

Market in 1990

Four firms, each with
25 per cent of market share

Market in 1991

Four leading firms,
each with 20 per cent
market share, but higher
sales than the previous year.
New small firms
(shaded area) have won their
market by taking advantage
of market growth

Fig. 2.7 Growth markets offer opportunities for new entrants

usually be concerned about a few new entrants. In fact, they may not even notice their existence.

In a market which is static or growing only slowly, competition is usually much more fierce. Like fish competing for food in an overcrowded pond, one company can make gains only at the expense of others. Firms often cut prices and offer incentives in order to hang onto their customers. As a result, profitability is often poor. It is far better, therefore, to aim for markets showing a high rate of growth.

Sources of information about markets. There is a wealth of published information about the size and growth of specific markets, details of which are in Chapter 5. A good way to get a flavour of different markets is to read brief reports such as *Mintel* or *Key Note* reports. Trade magazines will also give details of what is happening in their markets, and the broadsheet

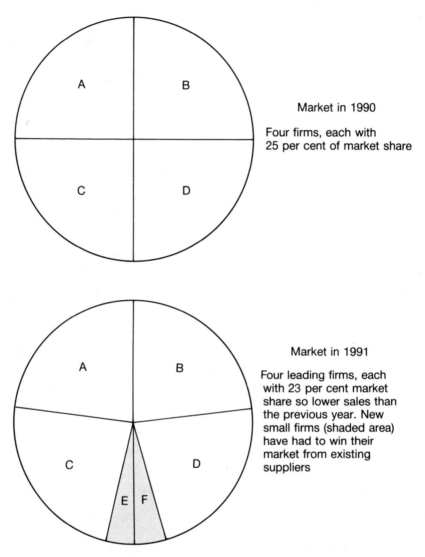

Market in 1990

Four firms, each with
25 per cent of market share

Market in 1991

Four leading firms, each
with 23 per cent market
share so lower sales than
the previous year. New
small firms (shaded area)
have had to win their
market from existing
suppliers

Fig. 2.8 Static markets offer poor prospects for new entrants

newspapers and informative magazines such as *The Financial Times* and
The Economist will also have regular features on different markets. Various
indexes offer a useful short cut to finding relevant sources of information.
The best are the *Reports Index* or *Clover Newspaper Index* for articles; the
Key Note Source Book or *Marketsearch* for published market research studies.

The competition

Whether or not markets are growing or static, some will display a more intense level of competition than others. Sometimes, growth markets are seen as 'flavour of the month' and become very overcrowded as a result. On the other hand, some markets, because they do not show such high growth areas and are possibly perceived as old-fashioned, do not attract the attention of larger companies. These markets may offer attractive opportunities for the small business.

Normally, it will be more important to seek growth markets, but the level of competition and the extent of the threat posed by individual competitors should always be taken into account when assessing the attractiveness of market opportunities. To evaluate the competition you need to do two things: identify the competitors, and gather information.

1 Identifying competitors. The first step is to make sure you know who all your competitors are. Make an alphabetical list. There are several methods of identifying the firms that should go on that list.

a *Scan adverts*. Consult all the media which may contain advertising from your competitors. This could include newspapers (local or national), specialist magazines, *Exchange and Mart*, or any other possible source. Scan these publications carefully, looking at the small classified ads as well as the large display ones. For some markets you will come up with a very long list.

b *Ask customers*. Ask a few customers with whom you have good relations whether they have had visits from any salesmen, mailshots from your competitors or telesales calls.

c *Ask suppliers*. Competitors often buy stock or materials from the same sources. Ask suppliers (preferably the delivery drivers) if they have had any new customers.

d *Trade associations*. Ask for a list of trade association members – some are available to non-members.

e *Consult the Yellow Pages.*

f *Directories*. Check the relevant section of trade directories such as *Kompass* or *Kelly's* (details in Chapter 5). There are also industry specific directories which may cover your market sector. Check in *Current British Directories* or ask the advice of your librarian.

g *Join the local chamber of commerce*. If yours is a local market, the local chamber of commerce is the best way of keeping up to date with all the local business gossip.

h *Walk the streets*. To keep an eye on local retail markets it is best to have a periodic good walk round. Look out for new shops but also keep a sharp eye open for any changes in the product lines stocked by existing retailers.

2 Gathering information on competitors. Having compiled your alphabetical list with names, addresses and telephone numbers, you have the basis of a file on each competitor. You now need to fill those files with information by taking the following steps:

a Send for literature. The first step is to contact all the firms on your list, as a potential customer, and ask for their brochure and price list. Telephoning is best because you can get an idea of how professional and helpful they are when responding to customer enquiries. If the competing firm is likely to know you and recognize your voice, ask a friend or an employee to do the telephoning. However, you would need a telephone with a speaker so you can listen to the conversation. If your phone doesn't have that facility, find someone who could let you use their phone for a couple of hours. It is wise to give a friend's name and address for the competitor's literature to be sent to.

You should do this exercise when you are evaluating new markets and on a regular basis with existing markets. You can learn a lot from what you receive through the post. Product lines offered, extras offered free or at moderate extra cost, terms of business, etc. You should also take note of the standard of the literature itself. It can range from the badly typed letter with some sparse information to the expensive glossy brochure.

b Shops. If you are a retailer you have to visit your competitors, so look at their display, product lines, prices, special offers and check out their customer service. If there is a chance of being recognized you would have to send a friend.

c Accounts. If a firm is a limited company it is possible to send off for a copy of their latest accounts, for a small fee. They are available from the following addresses:

English and Welsh companies
  Companies House, Crown Way, Maindy, Cardiff CF4 3UZ.
  Tel: 0222 388588 (postal enquiries only).
  Companies House, 55 City Rd, London EC1Y 1BB (personal visits).

Scotland
  Companies Registration Office, 102 George St, Edinburgh EH2 3DJ.
  Tel: 031 225 5774.

Northern Ireland
  Companies Registry, IDB House, 64 Chichester St, Belfast BT1 4JX.
  Tel: 0232 329984.

Accounts do not usually give a vast amount of information, but they show basics such as turnover and profitability. However, surprisingly, some firms do file more than the minimum information required, making their accounts quite revealing.

d Market research reports. Published market reports (see page 63) will usually give details of the most prominent competitors in the market concerned.

e ICC tables. Available for over 100 industries, these 'inter-company comparison' reports list the main competitors (usually over 100) in the industry and form them into league tables according to criteria such as sales, net profits, sales per employee, return on capital, etc. They are very useful for seeing how competitive an industry is. If all the firms are making very low profit margins the market will be very competitive and may be extremely difficult for a newcomer to penetrate. The reports cost around £200 but are available in many large libraries. Further details from:

ICC Business Ratios, 28–42 Banner St, London EC1Y 8QE.
Tel: 01 253 3906.

f Examine products. You should handle competing products, use them and, if necessary, take them to pieces. Then decide if you can offer something different and better. Likewise, try to experience competing companies' services and judge them from the point of view of a customer. Unless you really understand your competitors' products or services it is very difficult to form an accurate assessment of your own ability to compete.

g Market research. What really matters is what customers think. Carry out some simple market research to find out customers' opinions of competing firms. For example, who offers the highest quality products, the best value for money, the most helpful customer service?

Remember, checking out the competition is vital. It is only through thorough identification of competitors and careful examination of their strengths and weaknesses that you can accurately estimate the level of competition in a market and assess your own ability to compete effectively in it. Once in a market you must carry out competition checks on a regular basis.

Cost of entry

Assuming you have satisfied yourself that the market is large enough to accommodate your sales objectives, it has good growth prospects and it does not suffer from cutthroat competition, the next question to ask yourself is: 'can my company realistically enter that market?' A number of elements must be covered in answering this question.

1 **The learning curve.** How much do you really know about the technology, the product area and the way the market works? Would you have to invest a lot of time learning about these things, or perhaps employ someone with appropriate knowledge and experience? It is a big mistake to enter any market if you are not fully prepared to tackle it, because you certainly cannot afford to use customers as guinea pigs while you learn the ropes or perfect the process. The cost of going up the learning curve can be very high indeed.

2 **Accessibility.** How accessible is the market? How high would your distribution costs be? Are you sure it is sufficiently accessible for you to be able to offer a good level of customer service? Is it feasible for you to sell direct to the market or would you need to sell through distributors (see Chapter 8)? If you have to rely on distributors, are you sure that suitable ones exist, and, if so, that they would be prepared to handle your product? In overseas markets, in particular, the distribution problem can be a major hurdle to overcome.

3 **Getting your message across.** Some markets may not be crowded in terms of the number of companies competing with each other for market share but they may be extremely crowded in terms of suppliers competing with each other for potential buyers' attention. Many consumer markets are like this, especially those for fast-moving consumer goods such as

food, drink or confectionary. They are becoming increasingly dominated by a small number of large companies who devote huge sums to advertising and promotion. In this situation it can be very difficult for the small company, with a small promotional budget, to get its voice heard, however good its product.

Summary

Your objective is to locate opportunities in the marketplace which your firm would be in a strong position to exploit. To do this you should:

1 Start by taking a very wide view which you increasingly narrow down until you are focussing in detail on the needs of individual customers.

2 The wide view involves a scanning of the 'pest' factors of political, economic, social and technological trends. Your objective here is to identify broad opportunities and threats and to direct your information gathering towards opportunities and away from threats.

3 Broad opportunities in the environment lead to identifiable markets for specific products and services. In assessing markets it is necessary to satisfy yourself that:

a the market is big enough
b it is growing
c it does not suffer from excessively intense competition
d the company would not be prevented from entering the market through problems such as insufficient specialist knowledge, accessibility problems or the high cost of promotion

Action

1 The wider environment.

Column A	Column B	
Significant environmental trends	Possible implications for my firm	
Political trends	*Opportunity*	*Threat*
1		
2		
3		
Economic trends		
1		
2		
3		
Social trends		
1		
2		
3		
Technological trends		
1		
2		
3		

Fill in the two columns in the chart on the previous page for each of the 'pest' factors. In each case, try to think of three trends which are prominent and of some potential relevance to your company's activities. You will see that the second column, about implications for your business, is sub-divided into opportunities and threats. Some trends will affect you only positively or negatively, but it is not unusual for environmental trends to offer both opportunities and threats to a company.

2 Market opportunities. Select one of the opportunities which you have mentioned on the previous page, which, you think, could be exploited by your company. Answer the following questions:

a in general tems, do you think the market is large enough?

b what evidence is there that it is a growth market?

c what do you know about competitive activity in the market? For example: can you name four companies already operating in the market? What do you know about the intensity of that competition? Is there much price cutting, for example?

d if you decided to enter that market: what new expertise would you require? How would you get the product or service to the customer? How would you promote it to potential customers? Is it within your company's resources to execute these tasks?

3 Are you aware of all the relevant trade journals or specialist magazines for that market? Check them out in *Benn's Media Directory*. Many trade magazines are free of charge to companies specializing in that trade.

3 Buyers and their buying behaviour

Aims of this chapter

This chapter highlights one of the most important factors that the small businessman must know about in order to be a successful marketer: his customers and the way they go about making their purchase decision. In today's marketplace even a reasonably simple purchase decision like buying a packet of cornflakes will be influenced by a number of factors. For example, a mother may buy a particular brand because she believes it is healthier for her family, a child may buy another brand because of the size of the free plastic toy inside the packet, and someone else may buy another brand because they liked that product's advertisement on television.

To be successful you must have a good understanding of the people who influence the purchase of your product and to gain this you need to be able to answer the following questions:

- Who are the buyers?
- What do they buy?
- When do they buy?
- How do they arrive at their buying decisions?

These questions will be examined with relevance to the two major groups businesses would normally sell to: other organizations, and personal consumers.

Organizational buying

Most businesses do not sell to individual consumers but to other organizations. These organizations may be manufacturers, service businesses, retailers, government bodies or charities. They may sell the product on to someone else, they may incorporate it in the manufacture of their own product, or they may buy it as the end user. As customers, however, they all have one thing in common: they are not buying it for themselves with their own money but are buying it on behalf of their organization with its money. They will therefore approach their buying decision in a different way to the average consumer.

Who are the buyers?

In some small firms, buying decisions are made by just one person, often the owner-manager. More usually several people are involved in buying decisions. As many as fifty people might be involved in major purchase decisions in some large organizations. This collection of people is the 'decision making unit' (DMU). The more you know about the composition of your customers' DMU and the individuals themselves, the better. You should try to build up a picture of the kind of people who might be

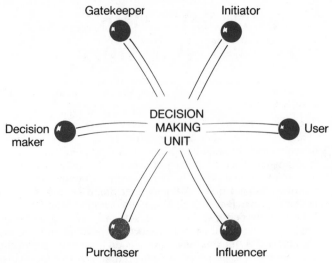

Fig. 3.1 Roles within the DMU

involved in the purchase decision and the role they play in the making of that decision. There are six possible roles and these are shown in fig. 3.1.

1 Initiator. Most purchases arise as a result of a suggestion from someone – the 'initiator'. That initiator could be an employee or it could be a senior manager. However, it is not uncommon for the initiator to be someone who is not employed in the purchasing company: consultants, accountants, architects, project engineers or other outsiders will often be responsible for giving advice that leads to an organization making a purchase. It is vital that you discover the likely initiators. These people will be important targets for promotional messages.

2 Users. The user or users of the product or service may affect buying decisions or they may not. Much depends on the status of the people who will use the product. Users of computer equipment, for example, are quite likely to have a say in its purchase. Many suppliers make the mistake of dismissing the user's role in buying decisions. Users can be very influential, and, if so, you need to reach them with your promotional messages.

3 Influencers. Typically influencers have very important knowledge or technical expertise which makes their advice very important when difficult buying decisions have to be made. For example, financial managers can be influencers. They may affect buying decisions by examining which option represents the best financial deal for the buyer, or simply by stating whether or not the organization can afford to pay the asking price.

4 Purchaser. Most organizations of some size will have one or more individuals entitled 'buyer' or 'purchasing manager'. Buyers usually have total purchasing authority only for regularly purchased items which are bought from one or more approved suppliers. Even in this situation, it is often wise to maintain relationships with other staff in the buying organization to make sure that everyone concerned is still happy with the product and customer service being received, because from time to time the organization may reappraise its links with existing suppliers.

Sometimes the official 'buyer' may be little more than a rubber stamp, filling in the paperwork for decisions already made by other members of the DMU, especially for major new purchases such as capital equipment. If you have not done business with an organization before, you should make strenuous efforts to discover who, in addition to the buyer, may be part of the DMU.

5 Decision maker. A common mistake is to focus selling and promotional efforts solely on the perceived decision maker within the buying organization. The 'buyer' is sometimes mistakenly cast in this role, but usually it is a more senior person such as the managing director or chief executive. It is true that in a complex purchase decision the managing director will usually have the final say, but this does not necessarily mean that he is the decision maker. If he does not personally have expert knowledge of the product or service being purchased he is likely to rely heavily on one or more influencers. In supplying the managing director with information, opinions and advice, they will be the effective decision makers. In such cases the seller would be well advised to concentrate his efforts on these influencers.

6 Gatekeepers. These people may affect your marketing efforts in a negative way: a secretary who chooses to consign your mailshot to the bin, for example. Similarly, a purchasing manager may decide to introduce you to an important influencer but, equally, may want to keep you in the dark about that individual and his role in the DMU. You need to make efforts to discover the identity of the likely gatekeepers and attempt to influence them to look favourably on your company, or at least to give you the names of all the key people in the organization with whom you should be talking.

What do they buy?

Back in the 1960s, the famous American marketer, Theodore Levitt, pronounced that nobody buys drills. According to Levitt, they buy holes. At least, they buy the ability to make holes. Currently, that usually means purchasing a steel twist drill, but it's not the drill itself that buyers want, but the ability to make holes. If a more cost-effective way of making holes (lasers for example) were available, buyers would surely turn to the new and better method.

According to Levitt, many great companies and industries have declined because they have not faced up to this question. For example, the American railway companies declined because they saw themselves in the railway business rather than in the transportation business. People were not buying journeys on trains, they were buying the most cost-effective way to travel to their destination. As cars, planes and buses became more cost-effective they began to turn away from the railways. Most railway companies responded to the increased competition by tightening their belts, trying to run their railways more efficiently and hoping to reduce their prices in a bid to become more competitive. However, although this might have made them more efficient it is no use being a very efficient producer of a product or service that nobody wants to buy.

Therefore, you have to distinguish very clearly between the following questions:

1 What business are we in?
2 What business are we **really** in?

The first question is an inward looking question and can be answered in terms of the product or service that you provide. The second question is outward looking, and to answer it you must put yourself in your customers' shoes and ask: what are they really buying? Define your business not in terms of the product you sell but in terms of the service that you provide for your customers.

Try to understand the customers' priorities when they buy a product or service like yours. Buyers usually also seek a bundle of benefits when they buy any product or service. For example, one would think that a steel stockholder is in the business of supplying steel and that the purchase of such a basic product could not be regarded in many different ways. But some buyers are really buying reliable deliveries of their raw material, others are buying guaranteed quality, others are buying the facility of last-minute ordering, others are more concerned about their tool life than about the steel itself.

You must identify your potential customers' priorities, not forgetting that different people within the DMU may emphasize different priorities, though, ultimately they will have to reach an agreement of opinion.

When do they buy?

Some buying is irregular, some is seasonal. Many organizations order products well ahead of the time they require them, others adopt a 'just in time' (JIT) approach, demanding regular deliveries only a matter of days or hours before the goods are due on the production line or the shelves. You need to be able to respond to your buyers' timing requirements.

For example, if you were trying to sell a new product to garden centres you would have to be ready with samples, literature, advertising and other promotional efforts in the autumn if you wanted to get your product stocked the following summer. That quiet period is when most garden centres make decisions about new lines they will order for the following season. If they decided to stock your line they would expect you to be able to respond to orders very quickly during the season. They would typically place orders on Monday, after the weekend rush, and expect deliveries to be made by Friday in time for the next weekend.

How do they arrive at their buying decisions?

1 Mechanical buys. Some buying decisions are virtually automatic. For example, when the paper for the photocopier is running out, it is likely that someone automatically reorders the same type of paper from the normal supplier in the usual quantity. This is a 'mechanical' buy.

Mechanical buys are typified by the following characteristics:

a they are very low risk
b they are usually low cost
c the buyer has experience of buying it before
d the DMU is very small
e the usual supplier is habitually used

This regular supplier is called the in-supplier. If your products or services are typically mechanical buys, you should aim to become the in-supplier with as many buyers as possible. Once achieved this position can normally be held by providing good service and maintaining close relationships with customers. It is much easier and less costly to keep existing customers than it is to win new ones.

2 Problem buys. Problem buys usually involve a lengthy and difficult decision making process because, perhaps due to lack of experience, perhaps due to the large amount of money involved, the buying organization is very worried about the consequences of making the wrong decision. Typical characteristics of problem buys are the following:

a buyers have no previous experience of making a similar purchase
b buyers seek extensive information from potential suppliers and other sources
c the DMU is usually large
d the decision making process is usually lengthy
e the purchase involves a high level of risk for the organization

The marketing approach for problem buys will need to differ considerably from that adopted for typical mechanical buys. You will need to make a very carefully planned sales and marketing approach tailored to the buyer's decision making process.

3 The decision making process. The following process represents a very useful guide to the kind of steps which organizations will often go through when making problem purchases.

Identification of problem
↓
Search for information
↓
Discussion of possible solutions
↓
Definition of solution
↓
Approach to suppliers
↓
Evaluation of suppliers
↓
Negotiation
↓
Purchase

The more thoroughly you understand the decision making processes of your organizational customers the more accurately you will be able to design strategies which lead to your company being selected as the chosen supplier.

a Identification of problem. All organizational purchases start with a problem. It is frequently the role of marketing to awake needs in potential customers by drawing attention to real, current, problems or by sowing the seeds of potential problems in buyers' minds by showing them attractive new possibilities which they had never previously considered. People outside the purchasing organization such as consultants, accountants, architects or inspectors can often be responsible for identifying problems. Hence, when designing your marketing communications you should always consider whether it is necessary to include people like these as a target audience beyond the buyers themselves.

b Search for information. Having decided that they have a problem which can be solved by making a purchase, the buyer will begin to look for information which will help him to decide which is the best purchase to make. Very often this information search will take place internally. Experts within the organization will be asked for their ideas, and trade journals, directories and suppliers' literature from the filing cabinet will be consulted. Colleagues in the industry may be asked their opinion as may knowledgeable outside advisers. For products or services totally outside the buyer's field of experience, potential suppliers may be used at this stage as a source of information, but usually buyers prefer to use more objective sources to help them form their own opinions before sellers are consulted.

c Discussion of possible solutions. Most organizations like to reach a consensus within the DMU about the parameters of the purchase before they speak with sellers. If possible, they draw up a tight specification of their ideal 'solution' before making a formal approach to potential suppliers.

d Definition of solution. Before they can proceed with a purchase, organizations need to reach agreement internally on precisely what is required. This usually results in a written product (or service) specification. If you are responding to enquiries from organizations you should always ask if they have a written specification because it offers ideal guidelines for your own sales proposals.

e Approach to suppliers. Usually buyers simply contact those potential suppliers who are known to various members of the DMU. They may have stored information in their files, they may scour trade journals or directories, but very often they go ahead on an incomplete survey of potential suppliers. In most cases, as long as they have a choice between three or four sellers, buyers will be happy. It is crucial therefore that your promotional efforts have made your company amongst those three or four suppliers that buyers think of first.

f Evaluation of suppliers. By this stage it is a dialogue between the buyer and the sellers which will shape the outcome. You will need to attend to all aspects of your relationships with buyers at this stage. You must respond quickly and efficiently to the initial enquiry. You must make considerable efforts to understand the buying organization and its DMU. You must be perceived as a supplier which is trying to solve its customers' problems rather than simply selling a product.

g *Negotiation.* In organizational purchases, the buyer does not usually turn his attention to negotiating terms until he has made up his mind about which is the best supplier for the job. He will want to be sure that all potential suppliers are offering roughly comparable value for money but he will usually be concerned primarily with identifying the company he thinks is most likely to provide the best solution to his problem. Therefore you should always give priority to building up the value of your product or service. Attempts to influence the buyer by cutting the price of your product may have exactly the opposite effect because it will make you appear desperate for the deal and thus lower the value of your product or service in the buyer's eyes. Always try to avoid negotiating until agreement, in principle, has been reached with the buyer. If the buyer is concerned only with price, and wants to haggle at the 'evaluation of suppliers' stage, he will make his wishes quite plain.

Giving away £10,000!

A very large multinational corporation in the pharmaceutical industry was contemplating the introduction of JIT (just in time) production management methods to one of its manufacturing sites. Part of this revolutionary change to their manufacturing methods would involve computerization of production control, for which software was needed. The decision making process was very long and the DMU was huge, because there were considerable risks to the company if the wrong decision was made. After lengthy internal debates and much advice from eminent outside advisers, a decision was made to go over to JIT methods. The cost of the changeover would be immense.

As part of this process, software needed to be purchased. It was difficult to find suppliers in which the buyer had confidence. The investment was so huge that the company did not want to risk problems because of gremlins in the software, or inadequate backup from its suppliers. In fact, if necessary they were prepared to write their own software, but would prefer an existing package because of the time saving involved, provided one of the software houses could convince them that their solution would hold no risk for the buyer.

Most software houses are relatively small companies and only one of the potential suppliers managed to convince the multinational buyer that their product together with the service and support that would be offered by their company, would be adequate. So the suppliers had been evaluated and the best external supplier chosen. The decision, however, was not yet made. The safety of the internal option was still very tempting. Further discussions were held within the DMU before a decision was made to go ahead with the external software house.

The software house was worried by this delay. Had they taken the time and trouble to really get to know their client's problems and fears they would have understood it. But they had not. They therefore assumed that the customer was undecided between themselves and a competitor. In a bid to clinch the deal they offered an introductory discount of 25 per cent (equivalent to around £10,000). For the software house this was a lot of money. For the buyer it was not a huge sum of money, and, more importantly, it made no difference to the purchase decision. Price was not the problem. Luckily for the software house, the large company decided to go ahead despite the price cut. The company won the order, but through failing to understand the importance of organizational buyers' decision making processes, they had thrown away £10,000.

h Purchase. The process culminates in a purchase order. It is worth stressing the importance of this piece of paper. Many small companies have gone ahead with work 'on trust', only to run into real problems later, perhaps due to a genuine misunderstanding with the customer but sometimes due to the customer deliberately taking advantage. Therefore, to avoid misunderstanding, all terms such as payment procedures should be clarified. Some companies, for example, expect to pay on receipt of monthly statements rather than invoices. To be safe, never make any move, however small, towards supplying goods or services until a written purchase order has been received.

Tenders

Tendering (or competitive bidding) is common in dealing with public sector organizations, in military markets, in the construction industry and with many large contracts in industrial markets generally. You need to ensure that you adopt a professional approach to tendering if it is relevant to your business.

If tenders are an important source of business for your company, you may find the following sources of information of value:

The Art of Tendering, P. D. V. Marsh, Gower Technical Press.

Tendering for Government Contracts, available from the Small Firms Service (*Freefone Enterprise*).

Selling to the MoD, available from:
  The Store Superintendent, Forms Depot, Ministry of Defence, Strathville Rd, London SW18 4QE. Tel: 01 921 2600.

Another source of information, *A guide to public purchasing*, covers tendering in the European Community and explains the proposed changes which will be introduced from 1992. It is available by telephoning the DTI's 1992 hotline on *01 200 1992*.

You should bear in mind some important points if you are thinking of going into tendering.

1 **Develop an intelligence system.** Devise a scanning system which takes in all the publications where tender details of interest to your company may appear. You should contact customers, trade associations and advisory bodies such as the Small Firms Service or the local chamber of commerce to make sure that you know of all possible sources of this information. The most comprehensive single source of information about public sector tenders in European Community countries (including Britain) is the *Official Journal of the European Communities*, which is available in major libraries or from:

  HMSO, 51 Nine Elms Lane, London SW8 5DR. Tel: 01 873 8409.

2 Understand the buyers. The more you know about the buyer, his problems, his priorities and the composition of his decision making unit, the better you will be able to tailor your tender document. Therefore, personal visits to potential customers to gather intelligence should be seen as very important.

3 Decision makers have preconceptions. Although you cannot usually sell your product face to face in a tendering situation (although there may be an opportunity for personal presentations by sellers), it is a mistake to assume that buyers make their decision solely on the basis of what they read in the tender document. They will often have opinions of the competing suppliers based on previous experience, hearsay, suppliers' advertising, PR and other marketing communications. Your promotional activities therefore have a very important long-term effect.

4 Tender documents should be immaculate. If your company is not known to the buyer, the tender document you submit may be the only evidence he has on which to form general opinions about your company. Any superficial deficiencies may be noticed and could raise questions about the professionalism of your company. Therefore, the presentation of the document should be given as much attention as its content. Services such as laser printing and binding are now readily available from high street print shops and should always be used for tenders if your company's own facilities are not quite up to standard. A corporate brochure is very important in this situation since it can add substance to your company's image. If you have any friendly contact within buying organizations, ask if you can have sight of a few out of date tender documents just to get an idea of the general standard of presentation.

5 Following up. All tenders should be followed up. In the early days your small business may fail with the large majority of its tenders, but it will have much to learn from the reasons for its failure. A quick telephone call to the person responsible for dealing with the tenders, asking who was awarded the contract and why your company's bid was not competitive, can sometimes be revelatory. For instance, you may find out that you have been omitting vital information from your document without realising it. At least you can begin to compile a 'bid history file' which will provide useful information about the successful and less successful aspects of your own tenders and may give you valuable insights into the decision making process of individual customers to whom you submit tenders quite often.

6 1992. It is also worth stressing that tendering will become even more competitive once the Single European Market is operational. From 1992 all tenders, including those in the public sector, will be open to bids from suppliers in any member country. This will present many companies with increased opportunities but also increased competition.

Consumer buying

The concepts discussed in relation to organizational buying behaviour apply in equal measure to consumer markets. Only the points which are worth emphasising differ.

Who are the buyers?

Although joint decision making is quite common in consumer markets, the members of a consumer DMU will almost always be members of the same family and thus the divergence of their views will be less than in organizational purchases. However, as toy manufacturers, for example, will be well aware, products often have to appeal to both the children and their parents.

In general though, individual buyers are much more common in consumer markets than they are in industrial markets. You will therefore need to build up an identikit picture of the kind of individual who is a typical purchaser of your product or service.

1 Sex. Is your product bought mainly by men or women? Don't forget that some products, toiletries, for example, are often bought, as gifts, by members of the opposite sex.

2 Age. Classify your typical customers into one or more of the following age bands. If your customers come from a wide spread of these bands, which age band covers the largest percentage of your customers?

0–23 mths	Babies
2– 4 years	Toddlers
5–10 years	Children
11–16 years	Teenagers
17–24 years	Young adults
25–34 years	Home builders
35–49 years	Family rearers
50–64 years	Affluent middle aged
65–79 years	Retired
80+	Elderly

The dividing lines are arbitrary but the general trends are not. People have different lifestyles at different ages and it is lifestyle which often determines which products and services they spend their money on.

3 Income. The following simple but practical groupings usefully qualify customers' spending power:

a poor: the unemployed, other people dependent upon benefit and those in very low paid jobs
b below average income
c above average income
d very affluent

It is reasonable to assume that around 80 per cent of the population fall into categories *b* and *c*, with more than half of those falling into category *b*. However, in isolation, income levels can be very misleading. They must be linked with other parts of the identikit picture. For example, Bob and Jim hold good positions working for a local authority. Both are 40 years old and earn £22,000 per annum. However, Bob's wife stays at home to look after their three chidren whereas Jim has one child and his wife returned to work several years ago and earns £15,000 per annum. The real spending power and the lifestyles of these two families will therefore be very different.

4 Lifestyle. For many consumers it is their personal priorities, their lifestyle, which determines what products and services they buy. Although lifestyles are linked to age and income they frequently cross those boundaries. Many people, particularly younger people, aspire to a lifestyle which is greater than their actual income or status. Where possible, they buy symbols of this lifestyle such as fast cars and fashionable clothing. Other people are much more conservative in their tastes and their spending.

People's lifestyles are also interwoven with their values. For example, some people are very concerned about environmental issues such as pollution, some people are very health conscious, some place a high value on learning and education, others are much more interested in having a good time.

So, age, sex, level'of income, occupation and area of residence may all tell us useful things about our customers but usually do not paint the whole identikit picture. You must also take into account less tangible factors such as people's values, lifestyles and aspirations if you want to fully understand buying decisions in consumer markets.

Try to come up with your own product specific lifestyle groups which look more precisely at the values and lifestyles of people who buy your kind of product. The example given in the case study below is one that has been used by Volkswagen in the UK. You can see how it enables them to focus on particular types of car buyers and to design advertising and promotional material to appeal to specific groups. All businesses operating in consumer markets should attempt to classify their customers in this kind of way.

Volkswagen (UK): grouping car buyers by 'type'

As a result of extensive marketing research, Volkswagen (UK) identified six basic types of car buyers in the British market. The following extracts describe their values and lifestyle in a way that Volkswagen hoped would help them to understand how these people might tackle the decision to buy a new car.

1 **Frightened.** Accounting for 15 per cent of all new car buyers, the main characteristics of these motorists is a lack of confidence in their driving ability. The men tend to be older, nearing or beyond retirement age; the women are often younger, with family responsibilities, and their fear stems from concern for their children linked to their lack of confidence in their own driving ability. Reassurance is vital for this group. Safety and reliability will rate very highly in their choice of car as will anything which reduces the strain of driving or makes it easier.

2 **Sunday driver.** A largely male group, they tend to use public transport to travel to work and thus use their car less frequently than other groups. Sunday drivers are more likely to be working in more introverted, planning and thinking occupations rather than extrovert based ones such as sales. Their most important reason for choosing a car is value for money.

3 **Small is beautiful.** Accounting for 21 per cent of new car buyers, this is the largest group. With above average income levels, they buy small cars from preference rather than economic necessity. They are not confident drivers and prefer a small car for ease of manoeuvering and parking.

4 Car disinterested. This group is basically negative towards cars and all aspects of motoring. They are not at all mechanically minded and do not regard the car as a status symbol. Middle aged and well off, they see the car only as a means of getting from A to B. It will be very difficult to attract their attention to advertisements and other promotional material.

5 Pro-Am. This group is the opposite of 4. Its members are interested in all aspects of cars and driving. They read the motoring press, advise others about cars and engines and have a secret desire to be racing or rally drivers. Almost all men, they are usually younger adults in skilled manual, clerical or junior to middle management positions. They are interested in engineering excellence, advanced technology and performance figures. Cars do not need to be flashy since exterior shape and styling are less important to this group than engineering.

6 Boy racers. Comprising 17 per cent of new car buyers, members of this group are aggressive drivers and see their car as a status symbol. 37 per cent of this group are female (girl racers), they have the youngest age profile of any group, are well above average wage earners and could be said to typify the 'yuppie' population.

In fact, the marketing research information was much more detailed than the brief summaries given above. It included more general lifestyle details such as social values, leisure interests and readership of newspapers and magazines. It enabled Volkswagen to build up identikit pictures of six typical car buyers and to develop marketing strategies to appeal to each of these groups.

What do they buy?

As with organizational markets, different people may buy the same product for different reasons. These reasons could include:

a product performance
b product quality
c product desirability
d fashion
e the reputation of the supplier
f price
g convenience of purchase
h good customer service
i good after sales service

It is vital that you discover the priorities of typical customers for your product or service. Armed with this understanding you can develop marketing strategies which make the right appeal to your target market.

When do they buy?

Many consumer purchases are seasonal. Other purchases are habitually made at certain times of the day, week or month. These timing factors can be of vital importance in the ability of your company to compete effectively in the marketplace. For example, you may have to produce and store products in readiness for high seasonal demand. This can have profound effects on your cash flow and needs very careful management.

How do they arrive at their buying decisions?

1 Low involvement decisions. Some consumer purchases are mechanical, often made on the basis of habit, convenience or necessity and given little, if any, thought. Such purchases include morning newspapers, petrol, cigarettes, an ice cream on a warm summer's day and even some more costly purchases such as a new exhaust system for the car or a plumber to repair the malfunctioning central heating on a cold winter's day. These low involvement decisions are not necessarily low cost or unimportant but they are made quickly. However, consumers usually buy on the basis of imperfect knowledge of the full range of products and services available. The question for you is how to ensure that it is your product or service which is chosen rather than overlooked.

2 High involvement decisions. Some purchases present consumers with great problems. It may be the cost of the item, for example, a new car or a foreign holiday. Sometimes consumers' lack of knowledge makes it difficult to evaluate competing products, such as a new hi-fi or a pension scheme. Whatever the reason, the buyer does spend time gathering and evaluating information before he makes the purchase. There are four key steps to this:

1 Identification of need.

2 Search for information.

3 Evaluation of suppliers.

4 Purchase decision.

The buying process starts with the recognition of a problem or a need on the part of the buyer. The more you understand about this first stage the more you can use your own marketing communications to trigger off the process by drawing the consumer's attention to the fact that he is not totally content with his lot and there are better products or better services that could improve his lifestyle. Once the consumer is actively looking around the marketplace, he needs information. Many firms make the mistake of not giving consumers enough information on which to base their decision. By the third stage, the consumer's information requirements have changed again. He is making direct comparisons with competing products. If you can help him to do this by providing appropriate data, you may gain an advantage but you also need to be aware of the objective sources of information which he may turn to (for example, *Which?* magazine). It is at this stage that your long running PR campaign really starts to pay dividends. Finally, by the fourth stage, the buyer is ready to make his purchase decision.

It cannot be emphasized too much how important it is that you understand this decision making process for your own products or services.

Summary

The success of all your marketing activities from designing and making products to promoting and selling them will depend upon the accuracy of your understanding of customers. This chapter has made a number of points which should help to direct your efforts to understand buying behaviour.

1 The behaviour of individual consumers and organizational customers often differs. If you sell to both, you should treat them as different parts of your market.

2 The first step towards understanding is to identify the buyers. In organizational markets there can be many individuals involved in a decision making unit. In consumer markets, joint decisions are less common.

3 In consumer markets the nature of individual customers should be explored, with the objective of building up an identikit picture of a typical buyer.

4 In all markets, the key benefits sought by buyers should be clearly identified.

5 You should also develop an understanding of the decision making processes used by customers so that you can attempt to influence them in an appropriate way.

6 For some companies tendering will be very important. If you submit many tenders the subject merits further study, but the adoption of a small number of common sense points can improve your success in this field.

Action

If you sell to businesses or other organizations, the following market research activities will be very useful.

1 Select a recent sale which you regard as an important success, and which you probably had to work very hard to achieve. Try to work out how your customer arrived at the decision to buy from your company by copying out a table along the lines of the one shown below and filling it in. In column 1, you should list all the people in the buying organization who, you think, had any involvement in their decision to buy from you. In column 2, you should label each individual according to the part he played in that decision not forgetting that an individual may have played more than one of those parts. In column 3, you should enter the most important benefits that each individual was seeking as a result of buying this product or service. In column 4, you should give each individual a power rating from 1 (low) to 5 (high), according to the extent to which you believe that person influenced the decision to buy.

Column 1	Column 2	Column 3	Column 4
People	Part(s)	Priorities	Power

2 Now approach one of the people you have mentioned in the above exercise. Ask if you can pay him a brief visit to help you with some market research. When you visit, take a blank form headed exactly the same as the one above. Ask your contact to fill it in. You should find it very interesting and useful comparing your view of their purchase decision with how it was really made.

3 Now undertake exactly the same exercise again, but with a contact from a potential customer where you failed to get the order. Compare your judgements of that situation with those of your successful sale. You might find the results interesting and informative.

NB Research visits of this nature are never a waste of time. Apart from your own learning process, valuable contacts are made and renewed, and it is from contacts like this that you often get business in the future.

4 If you sell to consumer markets, write a description (an identikit picture) of a typical customer, using the information given on pages 42-4. Which parts of your marketing package do you think appeal very strongly to this customer? Which aspects of your competitors' marketing do you think appeal strongly to this customer?

4 Market segments

Aims of this chapter

The following quote comes from a book called 'Iacocca', written by Lee Iacocca, who for many years ran the Ford Motor Company before moving on to rescue Chrysler. Talking of Henry Ford's reluctance to invest money in the development of new products for small niche markets (such as the family space wagon concept, which Iacocca went on to implement at Chrysler) and his preference for mainstream products for mass markets, Iacocca wrote the following:

> 'In my book, if you're not number one then you've got to innovate. If you're Ford, you've got to beat GM (General Motors) to the punch. You've got to find market niches that they haven't even thought of. You can't go head to head with them – you've got to outflank them.'

If Ford, one of the largest manufacturing companies in the world, has to specialize in order to get the better of General Motors, then your small business also needs to specialize. This chapter is about how small firms can use the concept of market segmentation to become more competitive.

What is market segmentation?

You can't please all the people all of the time. People are different, no two organizations are exactly the same. Therefore, customers, whether individuals or organizations, have different needs and priorities. If marketing is about meeting the needs of customers, then it follows logically that you cannot satisfy everyone by offering only one standard package to the whole market as no single product or service will appeal to everybody.

To overcome this problem, you must divide your customers into groups or segments. Each market segment can be defined as a group of customers for a specific product or service who share certain characteristics and priorities which help to explain their purchase decisions.

Market segmentation is based on customer buying behaviour. Using the Volkswagen example in the previous chapter, it is clear that Sunday drivers have very different characteristics and priorities than boy racers. Two very different marketing strategies will be required to appeal to these two diverse segments. However, this does not necessarily mean two different products: the Volkswagen Golf, marketed in very different ways, may appeal to both segments. The Sunday drivers my be attracted by the safe, reliable, good quality image of the Volkswagen Golf CL, sold at a competitive, value for money price and advertised in an informative, low key manner. The boy or girl racer will be excited by the Golf GTI or Cabriolet, fast, stylish, trendy and advertised on TV by sophisticated young people who exhibit the kind of lifestyle to which the boy and girl racer aspire.

How to segment markets

Segmentation involves the drawing of a number of different identikit pictures to reflect different groups of buyers. The way you segment the market should be unique to your company, because it must isolate the key factors which divide customers into similar groups *and* which influence their decision to buy your product or service. There are many criteria which can be used to divide buyers into groups. For example, you could divide consumers according to their hair colour: people with black hair, blond hair, brunette hair, red hair, mousey hair, grey hair and perhaps even no hair. All of these are distinct groups of consumers. However, the groupings must be based not just on visible differences between buyers but also on factors which help to explain their decision to purchase a product like yours. The 'black hair, red hair' method of segmentation is of no practical value (unless, perhaps, you are selling a hair care product!).

Key factors

To segment your market you should look for key factors by which your customers can be divided into groups. These key factors offer a three step method of segmenting markets:

Step 1 Customer descriptions

Step 2 Customer benefits

Step 3 Customer behaviour

The first step involves obtaining information about customers, which is fairly easy to do, but is likely to result merely in a description of basic differences or similarities. As you move through the second and third steps however, you are approaching the heart of a customers' actual method of choosing between competing products. It is worth noting that as you accomplish each step and go onto the next you will find that information becomes increasingly difficult to acquire and interpret.

Customer descriptions

In consumer markets, customers can be grouped according to their age, sex, income level, occupation or area of residence. Social class is often used, especially by newspapers and other media, to classify consumers. The most commonly used social class grouping is the NRS (National Readership Survey), which breaks British people down into six classes:

A: Upper middle class
Forming 3 per cent of the population, social class A covers higher managerial, administrative and professional occupations such as barristers, surgeons and top business people.

B: Middle class
10 per cent of the population. Most people in management and professional occupations are in this class.

C1: Lower middle class
Covering supervisory, clerical, technical and junior managerial positions, this class, which is significantly less affluent than the As and Bs, accounts for 24 per cent of the population.

C2: Skilled working class

Typically 'blue collar' workers such as electricians, fitters, plumbers and print workers, they are usually of lower educational attainment than class C1 but often more highly paid. They account for 30 per cent of the population.

D: Working class

E: Unemployed

Consisting of lowly paid semi-skilled and unskilled manual workers in factories, agriculture and service industries, and those living on benefit, these two classes, which are usually grouped together, account for around 33 per cent of the UK population.

The big advantage of these methods of segmentation is the relative ease with which the information can be acquired. In consumer markets you can ask customers to return guarantee cards on which they can tick boxes giving information on descriptive variables such as age, sex, occupation and so on. Advertising media (such as TV, radio, newspapers and magazines) define their clientele according to these variables and many research organizations will help you to target your customers on this basis by providing mailing lists of customers defined according to such criteria.

Customer descriptions can also be used to segment organizational markets. Government SIC (Standard Industrial Classification) codes can be used to identify different types of organization. These codes, which simply attach numbers to different types of industry, are used in many trade directories and in government reports and statistics. Details on company size and location are also easy to acquire from directories.

As a starting point, this is a useful step towards segmenting your market. For example, if you sell windsurfing boards it would be useful to know that most of your customers are males, over twenty-five years of age and reasonably well off. In industrial markets it may be helpful to find out that a lot of your customers come from the North of England, that they are small rather than large companies and that they are in high-tech industries. Such information helps you to target your promotional messages.

However, the process described so far is no more than a first step, because although it identifies where you have been successful so far it does not explain why you have been successful. You know *which* companies or individuals buy your products but not *why* they buy them. Knowing which customers buy can help you to target your marketing communications but you cannot develop a marketing strategy to meet customers' needs until you know 'why' customers buy.

Customer benefits

Your second segmentation step must therefore tackle the question of *why* customers buy. As demonstrated below, the same product or service will often be bought by different customers for different reasons. Only when you know those different reasons can you develop and offer the right product or service for that segment and promote it in an effective manner, stressing appropriate benefits.

A wolf in sheep's clothing?

At management training seminars delegates are often asked to identify two different segments of their market and describe the marketing methods they use to sell effectively to these two different groups of buyers. At one seminar, a delegate from a company making marine engines which sell to a range of end user markets gave the following reply.

'We have a number of segments but there are two extreme ones. One is the fishing boat segment. They buy small working boats which must be reliable and economical to run. They are looking for durability rather than performance in an engine. They are very conservative and their purchases are based largely on rational, economic criteria. The second segment our company calls the floating gin palaces. These are the luxury cruisers, small boats by marine standards, although their owners don't like to think so. As far as the engine's concerned they claim to be interested in performance and technical details although their level of knowledge is often not adequate to evaluate such data. Their real concern is the image of the boat. It is a place to entertain and impress. Everything must look right.'

At this stage another delegate commented that it must require two very different product and promotional packages to satisfy two such diverse segments; to which the reply was:

'Promotional packages yes. The floating gin palace brigade require a very glossy promotional package. The promotion must match their lifestyle and aspirations. The fishermen would probably react negatively to such treatment. They prefer basic leaflets covering the main technical details. And the product? Well, they all get the same one. The fishermen get the basic engine with everything it needs to make it go. That satisfies them. The gin palace customers get exactly the same engine but, as with the brochures, they get a glossy version, a highly polished chromium plated one to be precise. It shines and gleams and looks as though it goes very fast, and it impresses their on-board guests. That satisfies those buyers in the up-market segment. And they happily pay a very nice price premium for the gloss!'

Benefit segmentation enables you to offer customers precisely what they want and to promote those benefits to them. Information enabling you to identify benefit segments will be gained only through a very thorough understanding of your customers, acquired through close personal contact or a result of detailed marketing research. You need to know exactly what customers use your product for and you must identify their chief buying motives.

Customer behaviour

Having completed step two of the segmentation process you may be convinced that you have now segmented sufficiently to develop appropriate product or service offerings and promote them effectively to the right target segments. And you may be right. Further effort devoted to segmentation may not be cost-effective for your company. However, before you rest on your laurels, try answering the following questions:

1 Are all the buyers within each segment very similar in their priorities and buying behaviour or are there any significant exceptions?

2 If you were in a personal selling situation would you handle all the

buyers from within a particular segment in exactly the same way, or would you approach some buyers in a different way?

These questions may help you to decide if it is worth dividing the market into more segments. If you are a very small company you may need to further segment in order to identify niches where you may be able to 'outflank' your larger competitors. The information you require to take this third step centres on the customers' behaviour.

1 Organizational behaviour. In business to business markets you might look at whether they have a highly structured purchasing process with formal committees or whether a more entrepreneurial purchasing approach is taken. Secondly, you might segment between go-ahead organizations who are always prepared to try new ideas and conservative ones who purchase only tried and tested goods and services. Another useful split is between companies which require a lot of information and help during the buying process (perhaps they are unfamiliar with the technology, or they regard it as a high risk purchase), and those buyers who are much more confident, perhaps due to greater experience of purchasing and using the product. In identifying different ways in which organizations behave you can often work out how this will affect their decision to buy a product or service like yours. For example, many companies win orders from cautious buyers because they provide comprehensive written information about their product and are prepared to spend time with the buyer listening to his concerns and answering his questions.

2 Consumer behaviour. In consumer markets you will also be looking at the finer details by this stage, and these details can have an influential effect on your marketing plans. It is common in consumer markets to segment people according to their values and lifestyles. For example, people who are strong believers in the green movement will tend to buy similar, environmentally friendly, products and can be grouped together. There are commercial organizations who have segmented the British population using post codes and electoral registers. Their classifications, such as ACORN and Pin Point, offer very good ways of targeting precise groups of consumers, especially via direct mail. Mailing lists are often compiled on the basis of previous purchases. For example, it is reasonable to assume that the buyer of a greenhouse is a good prospect for other gardening products. Directories such as *BRAD Direct Marketing* provide comprehensive help and advice about such methods of targeting. More details of sources of information can be found in Chapter 5, and in Chapter 10 there is further advice on targeting customers through direct mail.

Targeting

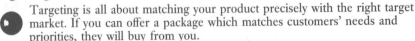

Targeting is all about matching your product precisely with the right target market. If you can offer a package which matches customers' needs and priorities, they will buy from you.

Three options

The three targeting options are shown in fig. 4.1.

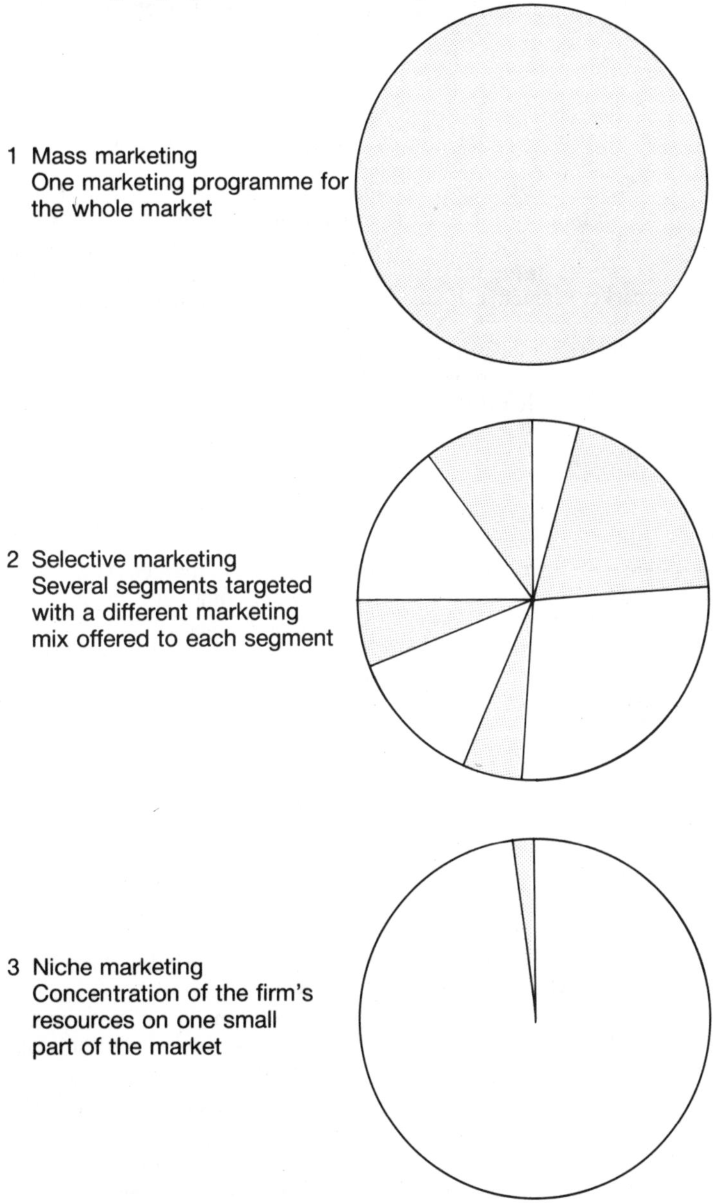

1 Mass marketing
   One marketing programme for
   the whole market

2 Selective marketing
   Several segments targeted
   with a different marketing
   mix offered to each segment

3 Niche marketing
   Concentration of the firm's
   resources on one small
   part of the market

Fig. 4.1 Three options for targeting market segments

1 Mass marketing. You could attempt to serve the whole market with a single product or service line sold in the same way to all customers. Products are generally promoted and sold to anybody who wants to buy them but the danger is that this 'all things to all men' approach will not match the specific needs of any segments.

2 Selective marketing. Mass marketing does not usually work in today's competitive markets. To be successful you must match your marketing as accurately as possible to customers' needs. That means developing different marketing programmes for different segments. If you do not have the resources to cover the whole market in this way, you must be selective and concentrate on becoming the best supplier to some, but not all of the segments in the market. You may decide to concentrate on two or three market segments. If so, you must offer a distinct marketing package to each segment. Perhaps you can modify your product slightly, or distribute it differently or promote it in a different way. As the case study on page 51 shows, changes to your marketing mix do not need to be costly, but remember that if there are different market segments there must be different customer needs and your marketing must reflect those differences.

3 Niche marketing. Niche marketing involves being very single-minded and concentrating all your firm's resources on meeting the needs of customers in just one small segment of the market. Many small companies start in this way, particularly if they are competing against large companies because it is often possible to identify a speciality area which is too small to be of interest to the larger company. If you are in a start-up situation, niche marketing is very appropriate as it gives you an opportunity to establish yourself.

Setting priorities

How should you decide which segments or which niche to target?

1 Level of opportunity. Firstly you need to satisfy yourself that the segment is big enough – that there is an adequate level of demand within the segment for the product or service you want to sell.

2 Compatibility. Even the most promising market opportunity is of little value to your company if you are not well placed to exploit it. You must match your company's strengths with the needs of customers in the marketplace. In looking for the segments which are most compatible with your strengths, you should ask yourself two questions:
a how well could we meet customers' needs in that segment?
b can we handle the competition in that segment?

Your aim is to identify segments where you would have a 'distinctive competence'. This means that your marketing programme would be different from and better than (in terms of meeting customers' needs) the offerings of your competitors.

3 **Accessibility.** Finally, you must ask yourself how accessible different segments would be to your company. For example, how easy or how costly would it be to reach different segments with your promotional messages? Accessibility is also about reaching your customers physically with your products or services. Can they get to you or can you get to them? People will often buy from the easiest place; they don't usually like travelling long distances. Therefore you have to look at the customers in each segment, compare yourself with the competition and ask whether it would be easier for customers to buy from you or from one of your competitors.

How many segments to target?

Having set your priorities, you have, in effect, ranked the segments according to their attractiveness to your company. The remaining question to be tackled is how many of those segments the company can realistically target. You must consider two main points.

1 **Resources.** Most small companies know that they do not have the resources to be the best supplier to all segments of the market. If so it is better to concentrate on being the best supplier to a few segments, even if that means reducing your attractiveness to customers in non-targeted segments.

2 **The cost of serving different segments.** Sometimes you can sell effectively to more than one segment at very little extra cost. The product may remain fundamentally the same, but the packaging or the promotion are tailored to suit particular segments. However, you sometimes need significant changes in the product itself to meet the need of different segments and may be tempted to stock more and more product lines to appeal to different types of customer. The danger is that you have neither the financial resources nor the space to stock so many products. If in doubt it is better to specialize. It makes financial sense and, provided you match your marketing with known demand in a niche market, it is better for your image in the long run to be seen and become known as the specialist in your field.

Summary

1 Customers differ. They have different needs and priorities. Therefore you cannot aim to satisfy all customers with one marketing programme.

2 Customers with similar needs, characteristics, priorities or buying habits can be grouped into segments.

3 You must offer different marketing packages, tailored to meet the needs and priorities of each segment you wish to serve.

4 Most buyers, if well informed, will choose the product or service which most closely meets their needs. The more precisely the market is segmented the more likely you are to match your marketing mix exactly with customers' needs in individual segments.

5 Don't attempt to cover all segments in the market. It is better to concentrate on those segments where your firm is best able to match customers' needs.

6 Several market segments can often be served with only one core product or service. It may be other aspects of the marketing mix, eg advertising, packaging, service, or delivery which enable the specific demands of these different segments to be met.

Action

Identify the main segments of your market and answer the following questions:

a can you produce an identikit picture of typical buyers in each market?

b what are the main purchasing criteria of buyers in each of your segments?

c which of those segments is most attractive to your company?

d what is your 'distinctive competence' in that segment? If you're not the best supplier, why should customers ever choose your company to buy from?

5 Marketing research

Aims of this chapter

This chapter is about collecting the information which helps you to understand markets and customers. To make sure that your marketing decisions are based on accurate information you need to:

- Have a well organized system for recording and using information within your own company. This is called internal information.

- Make full use of the wealth of published information which can help you with many of your marketing decisions. This is called secondary information.

- Fill any gaps in your information by carrying out your own simple market research. This is called primary information.

Internal information

Through keeping proper records, either manually or on computer, you can maintain an up-to-date marketing information system to help you with decision making. A number of very simple activities can prove of great value in building up a good internal information system.

Customer files

For most companies, the most likely source of new business is customers who have bought in the past. You should therefore ensure that you keep records of *all* your past customers, that these records contain as much useful information as possible and that you update them on a regular basis. This information will tell you what kind of customers tend to buy from your company and will help you to segment the market and target appropriate segments. Details can be kept manually, on cards in a card index box file, or on a computer, using a standard database software package. The exact details which you need to record will vary slightly from one firm to another. You can use as guides the two records shown, one for consumer customers, one for organizational customers.

Name
Address   **Post code**
Age   **Telephone number**
Occupation
Family details
Hobbies
Newspaper readership
Magazine readership
Most recent purchase: *item(s)*   *date*
Source of contact

Fig. 5.1 Customer record card (consumer markets)

Such details are not difficult to acquire. If you have direct contact with customers you can ask them to fill in a short questionnaire, or registration form, when they visit your premises. Even if you have no direct contact with end users, because your product is sold through middlemen, these details are still important to you. Registration cards can often be included inside your product's packaging so that consumers can return them after they have taken delivery of the product. If you sell unpackaged products to organizational markets through middlemen, you can often tag the product with your registration card inside a polythene bag. Companies selling to organizational markets will often require additional customer details, particularly the names of the product buying decision makers. However, you cannot necessarily expect to get all these details through your customer filling in a card. You may have to acquire some details later, perhaps as a result of a sales call or a telephone call.

Company name
Address   **Post code**
Telephone   Telex   **Fax**
Company size
SIC code
Contact name
  Position
Contact 2
  Position
Contact 3
  Position
Contact 4
  Position
Contact 5
  Position
Contact 6
  Position
Responded to
Previous responses
Literature sent
Telephone
Visit
  Visited by
  Date of visit (s)
Date of order (s)
Value of order (s)

Fig. 5.2 Customer record card (organizational markets)

Making the most of your customer base

Winner of first prize in the Institute of Marketing's National Marketing Awards in the small organization category (under £1m turnover) was the Polurrian Hotel on the Lizard Peninsular in South Cornwall. The problem it faced was that it was finding the low season periods of spring and autumn increasingly difficult to fill. With the help of a marketing consultant, the hotel's owners decided to tackle the problem.

The consultant was impressed with the Polurrian's comprehensive information system: record cards for 5000 guests who had stayed at the hotel over the previous 15 years. The owners had recorded extensive details of their customers, including, even, their newspaper reading habits. Knowledge of their guests family size, frequency of stay, leisure interests, etc, enabled them to build up an identikit picture of their typical guest, which in turn enabled them to target appropriate segments of the UK market.

Prime target segments were decided to be active retired couples who could take holidays in the spring and autumn and affluent young people in the South East who could afford weekend breaks and business conferences.

Before developing a marketing strategy, the Polurrian undertook a thorough competitive analysis. With over 900 'four crown' hotels in the UK and 43 in Cornwall alone directly competing with the Polurrian, the market was very fragmented and extremely competitive. The Polurrian identified 20 hotels in the UK which competed in comparable markets. Staff were assigned to monitor these competitors, visiting them, seeing their facilities and the services they offered and checking their prices.

The hotel then developed a marketing strategy which concentrated on prime target segments with the aim of offering a package which more closely satisfied their needs than any of the competitors' services.

Amongst the Polurrian's many marketing initiatives was a new brochure which attracted younger guests by emphasising the hotel's sporting facilities and older guests with photographs of couples enjoying walking on the local clifftops. A direct mail campaign gave former guests news of a new 'Leisure Break' programme, and later, special interest holidays for National Trust members, bird watchers, gardeners and health enthusiasts. A novel fly-drive programme was arranged with a local airline and leaflets were placed in the planes on the Heathrow-Newquay route. This also helped the hotel to tackle the business segment, as did an arrangement with the British Telecom International Satellite Earth Station at nearby Goonhilly enabling the Polurrian to offer teleconferencing facilities.

The Polurrian embarked on a clearly planned, highly targeted promotional campaign, and it worked. Average room occupancy in 1988 was 76 per cent compared with 57 per cent in 1985 and 50 per cent for West Country hotels in general. The conversion rate of enquiries to bookings improved from 1 in 20 in 1 in 6.

Information files

Most firms accumulate a lot of published material, such as competitors' brochures, old copies of trade journals, and so on. However, because it is frequently stored in a disorganized way it makes it difficult if not impossible to extract specific information when required. The easiest way to overcome this problem is to make one person responsible for 'information files'. That person should be responsible for scanning trade journals and other relevant publications on a regular basis, and be responsible for acquiring competitors' literature at set intervals.

The sort of information to be looked out for should fall under a number of predetermined headings, for example: new competitive products, new competitor adverts or press releases, acquisitions or mergers of competitors or customers, new legislation or other relevant political news, market information, technological news, new business opportunities, and tender notices. The individual responsible can then produce a brief summary of relevant information and its source, under each heading. This system has four advantages:

1 You can save your valuable time and that of any manager you employ. Busy people need only read the summary rather than plough through the originals.

2 The journals do not get lost.

3 When information is required, perhaps for planning meetings, the system enables it to be located easily.

4 This position can be an introduction to your business for a new junior employee.

Staff

Sales people, maintenance or service engineers, delivery drivers and any other staff who have contact with customers are your firm's 'eyes and ears' in the marketplace. They can feed back new product ideas, they can spot needs which are not being satisfied or are being met badly and they can obtain information on competitive activity. Staff should also keep brief notes of all customer visits as they will be very useful at planning meetings.

Street Crane: using staff to gain information

Street Crane is a manufacturer of factory cranes. The firm is based in Derbyshire and employs around 100 people, of whom six are sales representatives. Direct mail is an important method of generating new leads for the company, and for this technique to work well a customer mailing list is necessary. Rented lists proved problematical because only a proportion of companies in any particular industrial sector are potential crane buyers. Street Crane therefore decided to use its salesforce to develop and update its mailing list. Each salesperson is provided with a small mini-cassette player to keep in the car. When driving round, the salesman can evaluate a factory or warehouse's crane potential at a glance and, if suitable, can dictate the name and address of the company into the machine. In this way, the six-strong salesforce submits between 700 and 800 names per month for the database.

Secondary information

However conscientiously you compile and update an internal information system, it will never contain all the marketing data you require. Periodically, you will need to seek additional information from outside the company.

1 **Information directories.** There are vast amounts of published information but the difficulty is identifying published reports or articles of relevance to your business. There are a number of directories which can help you in this respect.

a *Marketsearch*. Subtitled *The International Directory of Published Market Research*, the directory contains 11,500 listings of recently published market studies for both industrial and consumer markets. For further information telephone *01 930 3638.*

b Marketing Surveys Index. Published ten times per annum, each edition contains details of new reports published up to the end of the previous month. *Tel: 01 640 6621*

c Reports Index. Compiled by Business Surveys Ltd, this reference index lists articles from business newspapers and periodicals as well as some general market surveys. *Tel: 0306 712867.*

d Findex. An American reference guide to published markets and business research, including consumer and industrial markets together with industry and company reports. Of particular interest to companies researching North American markets.

e World Sources of Market Information. A series of large, hardback books published by Gower, volumes cover different continents of the world. Each volume includes economic profiles of the countries within the region covered, brief details of published marketing reports and a section covering sources of marketing information available in the different countries within the region.

f A to Z of UK Marketing Information Sources. A very useful handbook covering market research surveys, government statistics, trade associations, libraries and computerized sources of data. Published by Euromonitor. *Tel: 01 251 8024.*

g Market Research Sourcebook and Business Information Sourcebook. A useful guide to the guides, giving brief information about a wide range of marketing sources. Published, with regular updates, by Headland Press. *Tel: 0429 231902.*

h The Key Note Source Book. With over 11,000 entries, the Key Note Source Book contains information about published market research studies in over 300 industries from agriculture to business services; from catering to water supply. For each industry covered, this guide also tells you what kind of information is available from five types of information source: on-line databases, statistical sources (government and private), trade associations, periodicals, and trade directories.

The Source Book costs £99.95 including postage and is available from Key Note publications. *Tel: 01 783 0755.*

i Finding and Using Product Information. Another book published by Gower, this is an excellent guide to information for those involved with technical products. Covering libraries, directories, periodicals, etc, the book also has detailed sections on patents and trademarks, standards and design, and sector reports on engineering, electronics, chemicals and construction.

j Current Technology Index. Scanning a wide range of trade and technical journals, and published monthly, this index simply lists articles under various industry headings. Very useful and very up to date. Published by Library Association Publishing. *Tel: 01 636 7543.*

k Index to Theses. An index to academic theses for higher degrees in British universities and polytechnics, it could be of interest to firms operating in swiftly changing technological markets. Divided into subject areas, abstracts give brief details of each project. *Tel: 0865 730275.*

l Clover Newspaper Index. A wide ranging index of articles published in British broadsheet newspapers. *Tel: 0767 27363.*

m Anbar Marketing and Distribution Abstracts. Gives brief details of articles on marketing management which have appeared in a range of specialist marketing journals. *Tel: 01 902 4489.*

n McCarthy Information Services. This is a subscription service providing daily or weekly information sheets summarizing items from leading newspapers and serious magazines. To subscribe is expensive, but good libraries will subscribe, and the system is well indexed, so McCarthy 'cards' can be a very quick way of locating information from recent newspapers or magazines.

o Market Research: a Guide to British Library Holdings. Gives details of the 2500 published market reports which can be found at the British Library. If you can't locate the index, their Business Desk will check the availability of reports in areas of interest to you. *Tel: 01 323 7454.*

2 Government publications. There is much official information published by various government departments, often freely available and often forming an important base for many marketing research projects. Bear in mind that government statistics are sometimes difficult for the inexperienced to use and interpret although you may find them in simplified form via a trade association or published market research report.

a Guides. Two guides are available. *Government Statistics: a Brief Guide to Sources* is a free annual publication which briefly describes the main statistical services. For your free copy, write, enclosing an A4 sized stamped addressed envelope to:

> *Information Services Division, Cabinet Office, Great George St, London SW1P 3AQ.*

The more comprehensive *Guide to Official Statistics* can be purchased for around £30 and is available from the same source or from HMSO branches. It covers all official statistics and also some non-government ones.

b Business monitors. Published quarterly (though some are monthly or occasional) they give output figures for a wide range of industrial, distributive and service sectors. Although very detailed, and theoretically, ideal for market size studies, they can be very difficult to relate to your own particular information requirements. A guide, available from HMSO, called *Business monitors: what are they and how can they help your business?* may help you in this task. Individual business monitors can be bought from the Business Statistics Office in Newport and advice on the statistics they contain can be obtained from the office's library. *Tel: 0633 56111, ext 2973.*

c Annual Abstract of Statistics. This includes summaries of a large range of official statistics covering most aspects of economic, social and industrial activity in Britain. It is available in most large public libraries.

d *The Warwick University Statistics Service.* They will find specific information for you from statistical sources and from more general published reports and articles. Their services cost around £50 per hour, but some tasks, which could take you days, may be accomplished by them in one or two hours. If you have a specific, urgent enquiry, this service can represent good value for money. *Tel: 0203 523251.*

e *Other reports.* The Office of Population Censuses and Surveys (*Tel: 01 242 0262*) produces various reports based on the ten year official census. There is also an annual *Household Survey*, a *Family Expenditure Survey*, annual *Social Trends* and *Regional Trends* publications, *Housing and Construction Statistics*, *Transport Statistics*, an annual report on *Household Food Consumption and Expenditure* and many, many more reports of potential value to marketing researchers.

If you require more details of government publications, you should refer to one of the sources mentioned in the 'Information directories' part of this section, or contact ('phone enquiries only) HMSO Books Ltd, *Tel: 01 928 6977*, or Central Statistical Office, *Tel: 01 215 5444.*

f *European Community information.* The Commission of the European Community (*Tel: 01 222 8122*) provides information on EC directives, standards and statistics and offers an on-line service.

3 Market reports. There are a vast number of specific market reports which represent a mine of information for the researcher, and finding such reports which closely match your requirements is best achieved via the guides listed in 'Information directories'. However, the following reports do also provide a good overall view of what is happening in many markets.

a *Mintel reports.* Widely available in many libraries, Mintel's *Market Intelligence* is a monthly publication with around half a dozen markets covered in each issue. The company also publishes regular reports called *Retail Intelligence* and *Leisure Intelligence*, market reviews and a number of *Mintel Special Reports* which are much more detailed but more highly priced. Reports are available on subscription or a one-off basis, and tend to focus mainly on consumer markets. *Tel: 01 836 1814.*

b *Euromonitor publications.* Euromonitor offers a number of useful publications with a more international perspective, such as *Market Research Europe* which examines consumer markets in specific European countries, and a series of reports on consumer markets in Africa, Central America and other difficult-to-research areas of the world. *Tel: 01 252 8024.*

c *Economist Intelligence Unit.* The Economist Intelligence Unit publishes *Retail Business* which looks each month at specific retail markets, new products and companies. It also offers overseas economic reports on many countries and some special publications on particular industries. *Tel: 01 493 6711.*

d *Key Note reports.* One-off reports on particular market sectors, Key Note reports are updated annually, or at least biennially. Unlike the reports mentioned so far, Key Note reports also cover industrial markets. The reports look at market size, trends, recent developments and future prospects. They also give financial details of the leading companies in the market together with other useful information such as details of relevant trade associations, trade journals and other reports. *Tel: 01 253 3006.*

e MSI. The MSI Database series gives concise reviews of a range of consumer and industrial markets in the UK. Based on government statistics and other published information they offer an easy to read guide to many markets. *Tel: 01 640 6621.*

These five sources of market reports mentioned represent only the tip of the huge iceberg. It is essential to check several of the guides referred to in 'Information directories' to ascertain whether information of relevance to your company is easily obtainable.

4 Trade directories. There are many trade directories which can offer the small businessman priceless help in his search for specific information. The main ones are mentioned below.

a Current British Directories. A very comprehensive guide published by CBD Research Ltd (*Tel: 01 650 7745*) who also produce *Current European Directories, Current Asian Directories* and *Current Australasian Directories.*

b Key British Enterprises. Often cited as the leading directory of UK company information, it gives basic company information, financial data, directors' names and functions plus total sales and export sales. Published by Dun and Bradstreet.

c Kompass. Includes details of 40,000 companies and a detailed classification of their products and services.

d Kelly's. With around 90,000 entries it is the largest listing of companies, but only basic details are given for each entry. It is of more value for the buyer than for the marketer.

e Major Companies in Europe. Contains only 4000 entries but considerable details are given for each one.

f Marketing Pocketbook. Produced by the Advertising Association, this is a small, low cost fact book containing much useful marketing information of a general nature. It costs £11 and is available from NTC Publications Ltd. *Tel: 0491 574671.*

g Benn's Media Directory. Details of over 1000 British journals, magazines and newspapers, plus broadcasting services, other media organizations and advertising agencies. An invaluable information source for the small businessman. Available from Benn Publications. *Tel: 0732 362666.*

h British Rate and Data (BRAD). BRAD gives details of advertising rates for print, TV, radio and other media. It is by far the most comprehensive source of such details. A single copy costs £105, or an annual subscription (4 copies), £265. *Tel: 01 975 9759.*

i BRAD Direct Marketing Directory: Lists, Rates and Data. A unique resource for companies involved in direct marketing, the directory contains a wealth of information on sources of mailing lists together with details of 1000 other useful suppliers, from mailing houses to envelope suppliers. Annual cost, for two issues, is £180. *Tel: 01 975 9759.*

j PR Planner. There is a British and a European version of this directory, the latter containing details of over 7000 trade and technical publications and almost 1000 newspapers in 14 European countries.

k Advertisers Annual. A large variety of general information on marketing, sales promotion, public relations, direct mail and advertising is provided in this useful directory. 7000 companies providing marketing services of various kinds are listed. Overseas agencies and media are also included.

l Exhibition Bulletin. A good guide to forthcoming exhibitions, it is available by annual subscription at a cost of around £40, or on a single copy basis. *Tel: 01 778 2288.*

5 Trade associations. Some trade associations are very useful sources of information for marketers. Some have well stocked libraries, relevant, of course, to particular markets, and some employ professional marketing researchers. Most have staff who offer a wealth of information and experience of their particular industry and are therefore well worth talking to.

a Directory of British Associations. An excellent publication listing all associations with brief details of their purpose and services, and containing an extensive cross referenced index. Published by CBD Research. *Tel: 01 650 7745.*

b Directory of European Associations. Also from CBD Research, over 9000 European associations are listed and indexed.

c Trade Associations and Professional Bodies of the United Kingdom. Smaller than the CBD directory, this one concentrates on trade associations. It also lists chambers of commerce, plus the UK offices of overseas chambers of commerce.

6 Libraries. Reference libraries in general are useful sources of help because you will find in them most of the publications and directories which have been mentioned in this section. Libraries which are of particular use to the small businessman interested in marketing research are outlined below.

a Statistics and Market Intelligence library. Probably the most comprehensive source of marketing information, particularly for those interested in overseas markets. It also has a comprehensive collection of UK statistics. Photocopying is possible, as are telephone enquiries.

1 Victoria St, London SW1H 0ET. Tel: 01 215 5444.

b Science Reference Library. A reference division of the British Library, it also houses the British Library Business Information Service. It has an excellent collection of published market surveys, trade magazines, directories and information on patents and trademarks. Photocopying and telephone service available.

25 Southampton Buildings, Chancery Lane, London WC2 1AW. Tel: 01 404 0406.

c City Business Library. Contains a good collection of UK and overseas trade directories, newspapers and magazines, together with statistics and market reports.

Gillett House, 55 Basinghall St, London EC2. Tel: 01 638 8215.

d Central reference libraries. Many large towns have good reference libraries. Amongst those of particular value for marketers are:
Birmingham Central Library *Tel: 021 235 4531.*
Glasgow City Library *Tel: 041 221 7030.*
Holborn Reference Library *Tel: 01 405 2706.*
Liverpool Commercial and Social Sciences Library *Tel: 051 207 2147.*
Manchester Commercial Library *Tel: 061 236 9422.*
Newcastle upon Tyne Business and Technical Library *Tel: 0632 617339.*
Nottingham Central Library *Tel: 0602 412121.*
Sheffield Central Library *Tel: 0742 734742.*
Westminster Central Reference Library *Tel: 01 930 3274.*

e Business schools. The leading business schools are often excellent sources of marketing information. However, an annual fee may be required for use of their facilities. Amongst the best stocked libraries are:
London Business School *Tel: 01 262 5050.*
Manchester Business School *Tel: 061 273 8228.*
Warwick University *Tel: 0203 48938.*

7 On-line information. This is where an immense amount of reference data on a particular subject is held on a central computer and access to this information can only be gained through a company or body with a computer terminal which is linked-up to this main computer: hence 'on-line'. Many of the sources of information listed in this section now offer on-line services, for example, the specialist libraries. Companies interested in this facility should check with individual libraries, associations and publishers of directories, reports or statistics.

A recent growth area of interest to consumer marketers is the development of 'geodemographics'. A number of businesses are now using information technology to classify people according to a range of variables like income, lifestyle, post codes and electoral behaviour. Although expensive, this data is useful for segmenting markets, locating appropriate target segments and for using direct mail to reach target markets. Retail location decisions can also be based on such data. Different firms offer different services based on databases of varying sizes, compiled in a variety of ways. Leading services are:

ACORN from:
CACI, 59-62 High Holborn, London WC1V 6DX. Tel: 01 404 8034

Pin Point from:
Pin Point Analysis Ltd, Mercury House, 117 Waterloo Rd, London SE1 8UL. Tel: 01 928 1874.

MOSAIC from:
CCN Systems Ltd, Talbot House, Talbot St, Nottingham NG1 5HF. Tel: 0602 410888.

The *BRAD Direct Marketing Directory* gives full details of these services plus many others. For additional details see Chapter 10.

Primary information

However extensive your internal information system and however thorough your external secondary information search it is unlikely that they will provide all the answers you need to develop your marketing strategy. To obtain all the information you need you will have to get much closer to customers through the use of primary research methods.

Surveys

The most common primary research method is the survey. Surveys involve asking specific questions which usually require short answers. Very often you need to undertake a more exploratory form of research, such as depth interviews, before you can be sure of asking the right questions in a survey. There are three main types of survey and these will now be described.

1 Postal surveys. This method involves mailing, or distributing in some other way, a questionnaire for which written responses are required. It is usually sent to a sample of buyers for completion at home or at work.

The advantages of postal surveys are:

a low cost
b total anonymity for respondents
c long, complex thought-provoking questions can be asked
d large samples can be used

The disadvantages of postal surveys are:

a the questions must be very clear and simple
b questions may be misinterpreted or missed out
c those who respond may not be typical of the whole sample
d long time lag before significant number of responses are returned
e response rates are frequently very low

A little creativity and a suitable incentive for the respondent can go a long way to boost the response to postal surveys. In business to business research the offer of a small incentive is becoming increasingly common. For example, respondents may be offered a book token or wine voucher. In consumer markets where a large number of responses is essential, an attractive prize may be offered to the respondent whose completed questionnaire is drawn out of a sack. In both cases, the response rate is likely to be significantly higher, and even with the cost of the incentive, the total cost of the research is likely to remain low.

Bowater Scott: offering an incentive

Bowater Scott decided to use a mailshot to generate leads for their 'WypAll' disposable industrial wipes. However, the marketing manager also recognized the opportunity to generate additional useful customer information. The mailshot enclosed small samples of the product which the customer was invited to try. He was to record his reaction on a reply card/questionnaire.

You can see from fig. 5.3 that the questions could elicit some very useful information. As incentives to return the questionnaire, respondents were offered a free 'WypAll' bench top dispenser full of wipes, plus entry into a prize draw. Response topped 14 per cent and the information armed the company's sales people with useful knowledge about their products.

To; Richard Sutton
Bowater Scott Corporation Limited

I have tried my samples of WypAll. Please enter my name for the WypAll Winners Draw, and arrange for me to receive my FREE FULL WypAll Dispenser.

Please help us to help you by simply ticking the appropriate boxes below.

We employ on this site
Less than 200 ☐ 200–499 ☐
500–999 ☐ 1000+ ☐

My responsibilities cover
Production ☐
Maintenance ☐ Purchasing ☐
Research ☐ Health & Safety ☐

Other (*please state*) ____________

We manufacture ____________

We use wipers mainly for
Wiping machinery ☐ Drying ☐
Cleaning hands, etc ☐ Polishing ☐
Mopping spillages ☐ Dusting ☐

Other ____________

Our wipers come in contact mainly with
Grease ☐ Water ☐
Oil ☐ Chemicals ☐
Paint ☐ Disinfectants ☐
Cleaning fluids/detergents ☐
Other solvents ☐

Other ____________

My lucky number is

Claim your FREE WypAll NOW & enter the PRIZE DRAW

To qualify for the WypAll Winners Draw your card must be completed in full and returned no later than 31st July.

Ny name is ____________

Title ____________

Company ____________

Address ____________

Postcode ____________ Tel no ____________

Following this limited trial I think the main benefits of WypAll are
Absorbency ☐ Durability ☐ Colour ☐
Non-tinting ☐ Versatility ☐ Size ☐
Disposability ☐ Softness ☐
Consistent quality ☐
Resistance to solvents ☐
No threads to catch in machinery ☐

Other ____________

*I had/had not heard of WypAll before receiving this package (**Please delete*)

*I am responsible for buying wipers/ wipers are purchased by

Name ____________

Title ____________

Address (if different) ____________

Postcode ____________ Tel no ____________

Fig. 5.3 The 'WypAll' questionnaire

2 Telephone surveys. This method is becoming increasingly common, especially in organizational markets.

The advantages of telephone surveys are:

a it is the quickest way to obtain survey data
b national and international samples are feasible
c easy identification of respondents enables later recall
d two way communication allows questions to be explained or verbal prompts used
e response rates are reasonably good
f interviewers can key responses directly into a computer, saving time on analysis

The disadvantages of telephone surveys are:

a total interview time must be kept short, meaning simple questions
b survey may be regarded as an invasion of privacy and participation refused
c in consumer markets samples are biased as they are limited to homes with telephones

3 Personal interviews. Often carried out by people with clip boards in shopping centres, or on a door-to-door basis, this method of gaining information is most suitable for the consumer market.

The advantages of personal interviews are:

a the interviewer can explain exactly what is required
b products, photographs or other stimuli can be used
c high response rates can usually be achieved

The disadvantages of personal interviews are:

a high administration costs
b danger of interviewer bias
c because respondents are in a face to face situation accurate answers may not be given to the more personal questions
d some people refuse to agree to participate in this kind of interview
e interviews have to be in tightly defined localities in order to avoid excessive travelling, which makes the method unsuitable for most organizational markets

Finally, two important points need stressing. Firstly, a poorly designed questionnaire will have a harmful effect on response rates and on the validity of responses. Secondly, your method of sampling, or selecting those respondents to be interviewed, must be accurate. Both of these issues will be covered later in this chapter.

Depth interviews

Depth interviews are carried out on a one-to-one basis, usually lasting for around an hour. They are most suitable for researching business to business markets. However, this research method is very time-consuming, so if you commission a professional to carry it out on your behalf it will not be cheap. With fees of £200 to £600 per day (depending on the size and prestige of the consultancy), plus expenses, a research study involving, say, 20 depth interviews plus a formal report could cost £3000 to £9000.

If you decide to adopt the do-it-yourself approach, thorough preparation is essential, plus the willingness to devote your own time to the project. Above all you need to work out a precise list of questions that you would like to have answered. Although it is better to make the interview a discussion rather than a rigid question and answer session, your list of questions will ensure that you cover all the necessary points. Questions will obviously differ according to your situation, but the brief guide below should prove useful.

Questions for depth interviews. It is always better to start off with factual, more tangible issues because such questions are easier for respondents to answer. As the discussion progresses and some rapport is built up with the interviewee, more difficult questions about opinions and preferences can be introduced. It is important to be aware that some respondents will not want to disclose exactly their current or expected future level of purchases. However, you can often get around this by asking a question such as 'If your consumption of stainless steel wire is currently 100 units per month, what would you expect your consumption to be in twelve months and in three years time?' With a little discretion it is usually possible to convince respondents that you are just trying to understand your own market and not trying to pry into their business.

In developing your own questions you should try to group them into the broad categories of 'what customers do' and 'what customers think'.

What customers do

1 What products do they buy now?
2 What exactly do they use them for?
3 How is this likely to change in the future?
4 Who do they buy these products from?
5 How do they place an order?
6 Do they buy at any particular times?
7 Who gets involved in the decision to buy?
8 Where do they look for information about the product? (if necessary)

What customers think

1 When making their purchase decision:
   a what are their criteria for a good product?
   b what are their criteria for a good supplier?
2 How do our products rate on these criteria?
3 How do our competitors rate on these criteria?
4 What improvements would they like to see in terms of products or services offered?
5 What trends do they expect to see in their own industry over the next few years?
6 What do they think of these new ideas we have thought up? (if applicable)

Observation

A third method of acquiring primary information is the observation of typical customers in the act of buying or using your product or service, although the ease of doing this will largely depend on what your product or service is. It can be very effective in certain situations. For example, you may observe the behaviour of buyers in any self-service or browsing-type purchasing environment. Are some items, due to their location or their display, receiving more attention than others?

Experimentation

Test marketing a new product or service can be a very cost-effective form of marketing research. This is particularly true in service industries where the cost of developing a new product can be quite low; lower, in fact, than the cost of a thorough marketing research survey to estimate the level of demand for such a service. A new service could be promoted along with existing services for a trial period with enquiries or sales being used as an indicator of the level of interest in the marketplace.

However, it must be stressed that this short cut to test marketing is not to be recommended for most small businesses. It can result in retailers being left with large stocks of unsuitable goods which they have to sell at a loss: a costly mistake for your company. Manufacturing companies would be very unwise to invest considerable sums in the design and development of a new product without backing their judgement with some objective marketing research.

Carrying out marketing research

This section will examine a step by step approach to carrying out marketing research based on selecting the most cost-effective way of arriving at the information you require.

Step 1: Explore the market

This stage is a familiarization process which involves absorbing as much information as you can about the market in which you are interested. A number of sources of information should be consulted.

1 Internal information. If the market in question is one that you already sell to or have been interested in for some time you should have trade journal articles, customer records and other information which will enable you to make a start on building up a picture of the market.

2 Trade associations. The first external information source to check out is the trade association. By consulting the *Directory of British Associations* it should be possible to identify organizations of relevance to the market in question. The directory entry should tell you whether library facilities or marketing research specialists are available, but if in doubt, ring up and enquire. You should then visit the trade association which seems best equipped to provide information. Once there you will probably find a number of published reports of relevance and copies of suitable trade journals. You should also find appropriate government statistics and you may find that the association has repackaged the statistics in a more intelligible form. Above all, you will find knowledgeable people to speak to, who will probably be able to answer many of your queries.

3 Libraries. In some instances you can achieve many of your research objectives as a result of visiting one good trade association. Usually, however, you need to investigate more than one source of information. It is essential to consult some of the information directories listed in an earlier part of this chapter to ensure that you have not overlooked any readily available sources of information. For UK markets you will not miss much if you check with *Marketsearch* and the *Key Note Source Book*, and the *Guide to Official Statistics* will tell you if there are any sources of government information which you should investigate. Never forget that the library staff have been trained to ferret out the sort of information you are looking for. You should always make full use of their help.

Step 2: Describe the market

If you have found statistics, published market research and articles from trade journals or newspapers which are of relevance to your marketing research, you should now be in a position to describe in some detail the market you are investigating. It is often worth writing a brief draft report at this stage, putting on paper what you know about key issues such as the size of the market, its growth rate, the intensity of competition, the key players on the buying and selling sides, any market segments which can be identified and the nature of customers' needs and priorities. This exercise will clarify what you do know about the market, thus enabling you to identify the missing pieces.

Step 3: Survey the market

1 In-depth discussions. This stage is about completing the picture by finding information to fill in the missing pieces. It is almost always preferable to begin this stage with some in-depth interviews. The people you speak to should be typical customers, but could also include other people with expert knowledge such as trade journal editors, trade association secretaries, consultants who specialize in the industry, or public sector regulators of the industry.

2 Provisional conclusions. You should now be in a position to list your provisional findings and conclusions. Some companies will leave their research at this point, working on the theory that a test marketing exercise would be less costly than undertaking the next research step. However, you should think very carefully before calling a halt to your research. There is no point in wasting the considerable time and energy you have already spent on your research activity, and the information you have accumulated so far, though it may appear to be comprehensive, is largely subjective. To be more certain of the reliability of your information it is necessary to carry out a more thorough survey of the market.

3 Survey. In carrying out a survey, four aspects are particularly important.

a Survey method. Weighing up the advantages and disadvantages of the three main methods (postal, telephone and personal), you must weigh up which is most suited to your own research purpose.

b Sampling. If you are investigating certain industrial markets the total number of potential customers can be so low that you could attempt to survey all of them. In other words you would carry out a census. However, in consumer markets, and in most business to business markets, the total population of potential buyers is so large that you could only survey a representative sample of buyers. Statistical sampling methods are many and complex but those wishing to find out more can consult the following books:

The Marketing Research Process, M. Crimp, Prentice Hall.
Marketing Research for Managers, S. Crouch, Pan.

For practical purposes, the phrase 'representative sample' holds the key. The aim, when drawing up your sample, is to ensure that it is a true reflection of the total population of buyers in the marketplace. In order to do this, the following factors must be taken into account:

1 In many markets, respondents are not all of equal value. Large users (or potential users) will be of more importance than smaller users. Ten very large users, for example, could have purchasing power equivalent to one thousand very small users. This should be reflected in the sample surveyed, with the researcher attempting to select a representative sample of large, medium and small users.

2 Industry type is another variable to be considered. A product could be bought by companies from a number of different industries. These industries should be reflected in the sample in the proportion to which they tend to be users of the product.

3 Geographical regions should also be reflected in accordance with their importance in the marketplace, unless the firm wishes to serve only a regional market.

4 There is a temptation for firms to choose their existing customers when carrying out personal or telephone surveys in the expectation of a more friendly response. This, however, results in a biased sample. Both customers and non-customers should be chosen. Ideally, the proportion of existing customers in your sample should be equivalent to the share of the market which you hold.

5 The job function of the respondent should also be considered. You may want to survey only design engineers if carrying out a technical survey, but a general survey would also require a representative sample of members of the decision making unit.

c Questionnaire design. Length. Whatever survey method you choose, there will be an optimum length of time for the interview, beyond which respondents will gradually become impatient, will not answer questions properly and may even refuse to continue with the interview. The questionnaire must be tailored to this length of time, which will not usually exceed ten minutes (unless an incentive is offered). You may not have time to ask all the questions you would like to, but foregoing some questions is preferable to reducing your response rate.

Clarity. Questions should be clear and simple. Technical terms or any potentially ambiguous words or phrases should be defined. 'Closed' rather than 'open' questions are usually more useful in this respect because ticking the boxes to a limited range of possible answers is quicker and easier for the respondent and provides more manageable information for the researcher.

Layout. A clear and spacious layout is vitally important. Many questionnaires are squashed up onto two sides of a card or piece of paper, either for reasons of economy or to make them look small. There is little that respondents dislike more than having insufficient room for their answers and a cluttered appearance will reduce the response rate. Ideally, the questionnaire should be piloted to test the suitability of the wording and the layout. Choose three or four typical respondents, ask them to complete the questionnaire, then go through the answers with them, making sure they fully understood all the questions and did not encounter any frustrations when answering them. The questionnaire can then be amended to overcome any problems.

Introductions. Interviewers' introductions should be polite and general. In industrial markets respondents will often want to know on whose behalf the survey is being carried out. If they request it, they should be told that the information will be supplied to them at the end of the interview, since disclosing the company's name beforehand might bias the responses given. You should also take care to ensure that respondents do not include any people who would be likely to pass information to your competitors about your survey.

Respondent details. You should ask for details about the respondent (and his company if relevant) to check the accuracy of sampling. It is better to ask these questions at the end of the interview since some respondents may be offended if they are asked at the beginning. By the end a relationship has begun to develop with the respondent and he will consequently be happier to give you these sorts of details.

As an example, there now follows a questionnaire for a telephone survey that might be used to carry out research into the buyers of polyester resin for plastic moulding.

1 Do you use polyester resin? .... YES/NO

If NO, terminate interview

2 Off the top of your head, could you tell me the names of any companies that supply polyester resin?

1 ....

2 ....

3 ....

3 I wonder if you could tell me what are the main factors that determine your choice of a supplier of polyester resin?

1 ....

2 ....

3 ....

4 Could you tell me whose resin you mainly use?

Main supplier: ....

5 Three well known suppliers of polyester resin in your area are GRP Resins Ltd, Polyplas Ltd and Moulding Supplies Ltd.
I wonder if you could tell me how you would rate these companies according to a number of performance criteria. Please rate performance as:

VG – very good   S – satisfactory   P – poor   VP – very poor

	VG	S	P	VP
Delivery reliability				
GRP Resins Ltd				
Polyplas Ltd				
Moulding Supplies Ltd				
Technical support				
GRP Resins Ltd				
Polyplas Ltd				
Moulding Supplies Ltd				

	VG	S	P	VP

Customer services

	VG	S	P	VP
GRP Resins Ltd				
Polyplas Ltd				
Moulding Supplies Ltd				

Salesman performances

	VG	S	P	VP
GRP Resins Ltd				
Polyplas Ltd				
Moulding Supplies Ltd				

6 Do you ever look at any trade magazines? .... YES/NO

If NO, go to question 9

7 Could you tell me any titles of magazines that you receive?

1 ....

2 ....

3 ....

8 Which do you consider to be the best magazine for information about polyester resins?

Best magazine: ....

9 Do you attend any exhibitions to find out about new developments in your industry? If so which ones?

1 ....

2 ....

3 ....

10 Do you ever receive resin suppliers' literature, price lists or other material through the post? .... YES/NO

If NO, go to question 13

11 Can you remember any such mailshots that you have received recently?

1 ....

2 ....

3 ....

12 What is your reaction to receiving such information through the post?

....

13 Are there any other good sources of information which people can consult if they want to find out about polyester resins?

....

14 Are there any further points that you think should be made about the purchase of polyester resin?

....

Thank you very much, Mr .... for helping me out with this survey. I wonder if you could give me a few additional details to help me to analyse my data?

Could you tell me your job title? ....

The approximate number of employees in your firm? ....

Finally, do any other people in your company get involved at any time in the decision to purchase polyester resin? What would their job functions be? (*For each person mentioned, ask what role he plays in the decision making.*)

1 ....

2 ....

3 ....

Thank you very much indeed Mr....................

That questionnaire is just about as long as you would want to make a telephone questionnaire. Most of the answers to the questions are easy and short. You will notice that instructions have been provided for the interviewer, but even so, if you delegate the interviewing you should be in attendance for the first five interviews in order to ensure that the questions are being asked and answered properly.

The final point about questionnaire design is that the researcher should always allow for additional, unanticipated information. A question like number 14 on the sample questionnaire should always be included at the end. It will occasionally yield some very informative answers. With practice, you can often turn the interview into a conversation, encouraging the respondent to part with far more information than the bare answers to the questions. The design of the questionnaire should therefore leave plenty of white space for jotting down such snippets, which will sometimes be of great value.

d Analysis. Unless you are undertaking very large surveys, you will not gain much from using a computer to analyse the data. For example, analysing 100 responses to the questionnaire just shown need not take much more than a day. Let's now examine how you would go about doing this.

Targeting. The first question was obviously a qualifying question. There is no point in questioning someone who has absolutely no interest in the product.

Awareness. Question 2 was an unprompted recall question, designed to identify those companies which buyers think of first – an important pointer because the customer would probably turn to this company first if he wanted to actually buy the polyester resin. In analysis one would want to produce a league table of awareness. If you assume that those companies mentioned first were more prominent in the mind of the respondent you could award 3 points to companies mentioned first, 2 points to companies mentioned second and 1 point to other companies, and produce an awareness league table on that basis. If your company is not near the top of that league table – you need to promote yourself more strongly.

Purchase criteria. Question 3 was an open-ended question. Analysis would have been made easier had it been a closed question with respondents asked to rate the importance of various factors leading to their purchase decision. However, problems often arise with the difficulty that respondents experience in actually grading their own purchase criteria. Therefore, simply asking them to place their buying criteria in order of importance to them usually works better. The first step in analysing these responses is to code respondents' stated criteria into a number of categories, such as quality of product, or reliability of deliveries. You can then award points from 3 for most important criteria down to 1 for third (and any subsequent) criteria, and produce a league table of buying criteria. This is the most time-consuming of analytical tasks, but this should not deter you from asking open-ended questions if they are likely to produce a better or more detailed response.

Main supplier. Another league table can be produced from the responses to question 4. Though hardly an accurate picture of market share, it does give some indication of which suppliers are performing most successfully in the marketplace. However, in many industrial markets uncovering data about market share will be virtually impossible as respondents are often unwilling to disclose specific volumes of purchase from individual suppliers. A persistent attempt to obtain such information may sabotage the whole survey.

Competitive analysis. A question like number 5 can unearth some very useful data. If it is properly explained beforehand, respondents will not experience difficulty answering such a question. You will note that only four options are offered. As well as simplifying the range of choices, the even number does not allow respondents to take the easy route of choosing the middle option (for example, 'average'). In order to analyse this data you need to change the qualifying words (which were used to make life easier for respondents) into numbers, in this case ranging from 4 to 1. It is then possible to produce a league table for each of the elements of competitive performance. In this way you can identify which supplier is seen by customers as being the most reliable on delivery, and which as being the least reliable, and so on. By matching these tables with the data from question 3, much can be learnt about how your company rates on the criteria which are important to buyers in the marketplace.

One additional point needs to be made about analysing question 5. It is likely that some respondents will not know suppliers sufficiently well to grade them on all criteria. If this is the case, you cannot produce a meaningful competitive performance league table by simply adding up the scores. Therefore an average of the marks received by each supplier for each criterion would need to be made, and the league table compiled according to those average scores. Of course, if your company suffers from too many blank spaces in question 5, your image in the marketplace is obviously weak, illustrating the need for a vigorous promotional campaign.

Sources of information. The majority of the rest of the questionnaire is devoted to finding out the sources of information of the person being questioned. The results are obviously very useful for your business as they illustrate the areas to which your future promotional campaigns should be targeted.

1 Trade magazines. Analysis here is straightforward, From question 6, you can find out what proportion of potential customers cannot be reached at all through advertising in the trade press. Question 7 tells you the full range of journals that people consult. This is useful for targeting press releases though in some markets, building and construction, for example, the results would produce a list of far too many titles for advertising in them to be considered worthwhile. It is useful therefore to produce a league table of the most received journal and target advertising towards this. For other trades, however, a clear favourite will emerge. A telephone survey of plastic moulders, for example, found that over 90 per cent received *Plastics and Rubber Weekly*. Question 8 can be analysed in a straightforward way, and can be useful in identifying whether the most read journal differs from the most received, with important consequences for the targeting of advertising and PR material.

2 Exhibitions. A simple league table of exhibition attendance by your potential customers can be developed. If the results show that they are an important factor in influencing or informing the customer then you could consider attending the exhibition as part of your next promotional campaign. However, analyse the results carefully. Many companies waste huge amounts of time and money taking space at exhibitions via which they will reach only a small proportion of their target market.

3 Direct mail. Some markets and some individuals are more swamped by direct mail than others. Many people below director level do not receive vast quantities of direct mail and question 10 may confirm this. The answers to this question will also show that literature is often badly targeted, or not targeted at all, and is often of little relevance to the company. In addition, it is useful to know whether customers are receiving a surfeit of direct mail from polyester resin suppliers or whether they receive virtually none (a promotional opportunity). Question 12 is designed to ascertain whether they do read, store in the appropriate filing cabinet or even respond to, those mailshots which are relevant.

4 Other sources. Answers to question 13 may reveal some interesting promotional opportunities, such as directories, seminars and local newspapers.

Information about the respondent. Respondents should be analysed according to any variables which might be useful for segmentation purposes. These may be type of industry, location, company size or something to do with their internal purchasing procedures. The number of people in decision making units can be tabulated, as can the job titles of those participating in the DMU. It is then useful to break down some of the information from earlier questions according to these segmentation possibilities. For example, does the awareness rating vary according to different regions? Do purchase criteria vary according to end user type, or size of company? Is there any pattern in the kind of companies which rate the firm highly against competitors and those which rate it poorly? The information produced by a survey of this nature can be invaluable in segmenting your market.

External assistance

So far in this chapter it has been assumed that you would carry out your own market research. Many firms do this, but some do not have the time, resources or expertise to do so, and must therefore turn to sources of outside help.

Using consultants

Using an experienced consultant can often benefit the company because the consultant will add objectivity as well as expertise to the research project. However, some companies are disappointed with the results of such an exercise. When this occurs, it is almost invariably because the client did not select the consultant properly or did not brief him properly.

1 **Selecting consultants.** There are a large number of firms offering marketing consultancy services but no acceptable approval system which would guarantee professional competence. There are lists of consultants which are available from various sources, such as the Institute of Marketing (*Tel: 0628 524922*), the Market Research Society (*Tel: 01 235 4709*) or the Industrial Market Research Association (*Tel: 0543 263448*). However, these are only lists and cannot guarantee the suitability of the consultant for your purposes.

It is better therefore to find a consultant through personal contact or personal recommendation. Knowing that the consultant has done a good job for a friend, colleague or industry contact is probably the best recommendation. If the consultant does have to be chosen from a list, a number of pertinent questions can be asked. Does the consultant have any formal qualifications such as a marketing degree or the diploma of the Institute of Marketing or the Market Research Society? (*NB* Being a member of one of these organizations is *not* the same as having passed their diploma examinations.) Has the consultant carried out any research which is similar to the task which you wish to undertake? If so, is he willing to provide client names and contact names who can vouch for a good job done? Perhaps he can show you some tangible evidence in the form of reports written or more practical outcomes such as promotional campaigns developed as a result of his research. Unless the technology of your product is extremely complex, experience in your industry will be less important than the consultant's marketing expertise.

2 **Working with consultants.** The outcome of any consultancy project should be based upon genuine teamwork, involving a pooling of the consultant's experience and expertise in marketing and your own knowledge of the industry and your company. Fundamental in developing this joint approach, with both sides fully committed to the project, is a clear brief which spells out exactly what you want to achieve as a result of the assignment and exactly how the consultant will spend his time in order to achieve it. Both sides must be clear about the objectives of the project, and you must be happy with the way the consultant's rather expensive time is to be used. Fees and expenses should also, of course, be clearly defined.

Once the project is underway, regular meetings will help to keep you in touch with what the consultant is doing. You may want to get involved in the consultant's work for your own educational benefit. For example, you may observe market research interviews or make a visit with the consultant to a major library or trade association. You should certainly ask the consultant to reference all sources of information so that you will know where to find updates of statistics and reports in the future. At the end of the project, the report should be made available to you well ahead of a formal presentation by the consultant, so that you have time to absorb the findings and recommendations before discussing them at this final meeting. If there is anything you don't understand or anything you are not happy with you should raise it at the meeting. Consultants are well paid professionals who should not be afraid of having their work put under the microscope.

Other sources of outside help

Colleges, polytechnics and business schools can also be useful sources of outside help for projects of varying difficulty. Your local technical college, for example, may have students following business courses who would be available for short, project based assignments. Suitable assignments could include carrying out fieldwork for marketing research surveys, especially in consumer markets, where teams of people with clipboards are often required. The students may also be able to analyse and collate the results of their survey.

Polytechnics or universities with undergraduates following business studies or marketing degrees may have individual students or small groups available for more challenging research projects. Studies in organizational markets can often be carried out, as well as a certain amount of primary research. These sorts of projects will cost little, sometimes even nothing, but it must be borne in mind that undergraduate students are still learning and will be reasonably inexperienced and, consequently, their efforts should not be compared with those of a professional consultant. Of more interest to some firms will be the fact that students following a sandwich degree have to undertake an industrial placement for one year (or sometimes two six month periods) during which time they work for a company in return for a salary (£6000 to £8000 seems to be average). Firms with projects requiring lengthier research may be able to take advantage of these sandwich degree placements.

At the most skilful end of the scale are students taking Masters degrees at well known university business schools. They may have to undertake a commercial project as part of their degree, and may be allocated to companies for this purpose. Some students will be specializing in marketing and can be expected to undertake very sophisticated research projects, though their intellectual abilities will usually outstrip their practical experience. Fees or salaries will often have to be paid for these services but they will be lower than those charged by a professional consultant. University business schools who may have students available for such work include Bradford, Durham, Lancaster, London, Manchester, Stirling, Strathclyde and Warwick.

However, do remember that the average consultant has much more experience than the average student and it may be that if financial assistance can be secured to help with the consultant's bill, the professional approach will prove more cost-effective.

Grants for marketing

The Marketing Initiative

Designed to help companies undertake a thorough marketing review and develop a marketing strategy, the scheme offers to subsidize half the consultant's fee, and up to two thirds of his fee in some parts of the country. Up to 15 days consultancy can be subsidized in this way. If you are considering bringing in outside help, this scheme should always be your first step. The initial approach should be made to your local DTI office (*Tel: 0800 500 200* for information booklet).

The Export Marketing Research Scheme

Run by the DTI, the scheme offers professional advice on how to set about researching overseas markets, and then, once a specific overseas marketing research project has been decided on, up to half the cost of carrying out the project up to a maximum cost of £20,000 (*Tel: 01 215 4979*). There is much more help for exporters, details of which can be found in the companion volume *Successful Exporting for Small Businesses*, or from the DTI Export Initiative booklet (*Tel: 01 215 0574*).

Business Growth Training

This is a scheme run by the Department of Employment through the Training Agency (formerly the MSC), aimed at helping firms to achieve their growth targets. There are five tiers to the scheme, but the third one, Managing Business Change, is particularly appropriate to matters discussed in Chapters 5 and 6 of this book. Although the scheme involves training it also allows for the use of consultants to help advise the company through its period of growth. The scheme covers a one year period (whereas the Marketing Initiative must be completed in eight weeks) and is therefore particularly useful for firms wishing to develop and implement marketing strategies. The scheme will pay half the cost of using consultants and outside training facilities, and a maximum grant of £15,000 is available from the Training Agency for this purpose.

It is important to note that schemes are subject to change so you should check details with the organizations listed above.

Summary

1 The starting point for your marketing research should be the exploitation of your company's own internal information, found in the firm's records, its filing cabinet, its computer and its staff.

2 Outside your company there is an enormous amount of useful secondary information. By consulting suitable information directories and visiting the right libraries or trade associations you will almost certainly be able to find useful statistics, reports and other detailed information about your market.

3 To develop a real understanding of customers, however, primary research methods usually need to be employed. Primary research surveys are not cheap, so if they are to be carried out they should be done properly, without attempting to cut corners.

4 Using an outside consultant, carefully selected and properly briefed, will often help you to get value for money out of your research budget, and grants are available to subsidize the cost of this outside help.

Action

This chapter has discussed a number of very easy steps which you could take towards improving your information about your marketplace. Below are several measures which you could implement almost immediately if you do not already practise them.

1 Do you keep detailed customer record cards of the kind shown in figs. 5.1 and 5.2? If not, purchase a large card index box, place records for all new customers onto the cards and draw up a schedule for transferring as many as possible of your old customers onto the new system. You can telephone them, if necessary, for the additional information, and the call will act as a useful means of maintaining your company profile.

2 If you employ any staff who have significant contact with customers (including yourself), draw up a form enabling them to report back any customers' changes (for example, personnel moves) and any other news of interest.

3 Do you have one place, one filing cabinet or drawer, where you store relevant information about your markets and your customers? If not, allocate one for this purpose.

4 Is one person in your company responsible for scanning trade journals, newspapers, government publications, and so on for any legislative, economic, market and customer developments of relevance to your company? If not, make somebody responsible for keeping your marketing information system up to date.

5 Have you investigated the government grants? If not, ring *0800 500 200* for your introductory booklet giving details of these.

6 Writing a marketing plan

Aims of this chapter

Success in business is closely linked with the ability to plan ahead. There are two important aspects of this planning process: the ability to recognize and develop the most appropriate strategy for your company, and the firm's ability and willingness to pursue that strategy. The formal planning procedures outlined in this chapter will help your company to devise the right strategy and to implement it successfully.

The planning cycle

Time horizons

You can think of the planning cycle as having two levels, or as occurring over two different time horizons, as shown in fig. 6.1. The longer time horizon covers *strategic* aspects of the marketing plan: the marketing strategies to be pursued to achieve the firm's broad longer term objectives. For most small firms this will probably look ahead over a three year period. However, the length of this strategy period should be determined by the nature of the business and the market. For example, three years for an organization in a slow moving, capital intensive industry may not be long enough, but in rapidly changing markets such as fashion markets this may be too long.

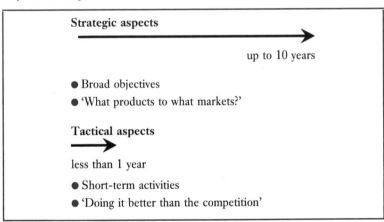

Strategic aspects

up to 10 years

- Broad objectives
- 'What products to what markets?'

Tactical aspects

less than 1 year

- Short-term activities
- 'Doing it better than the competition'

Fig. 6.1 Time horizons for marketing planning

Short-term *tactical* planning looks generally ahead over the next year, and in great detail over the next three months. Unless you are prepared to spend a little time preparing a detailed marketing action plan you will work very inefficiently on a day-to-day basis.

Strategic aspects

The aim of strategic planning is to specify long-term goals and then to determine courses of action and to allocate the firm's resources so that these goals can be met. Marketing strategy can be summarized as:

To achieve our goals, what products (services) do we need to sell, to what markets, in what quantities?

A later section of this chapter will tackle the problem of 'what products to what markets?'

Tactical aspects

It is the efficient implementation of the short-term activities which enables the firm to make sales in the marketplace and deliver satisfaction to its customers. Tactical aspects of the marketing plan are concerned with:

How will we implement our marketing strategy better than our competitors?

Doing it better than the competition involves detailed plans that cover each of the four main operating areas of the marketing process: product, price, place and promotion (the 'marketing mix'). The writing of the tactical plan will be covered later, and more detailed ideas for doing it better than the competition in all four areas of the marketing mix will be presented in Chapters 7 to 10.

Planning steps

There are four basic steps to planning anything, which are shown in fig. 6.2. Asking the right questions is fundamental to taking the right steps.

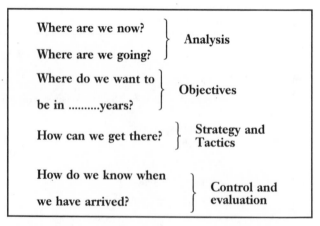

Fig. 6.2 The four planning steps: asking the right questions

In order to illustrate these planning steps in practice, they will be shown with relevance to a real life company, Prince Components, who are manufacturers of components to several industries.

Analysis

The first step in the planning process is to analyse the firm's current marketing position. This is sometimes termed a 'marketing audit'. Just as an accountant has a set of rules, or framework to help him to produce an accurate financial picture of your company, you should also have a method for assessing your company's marketing situation. This is known as a SWOT analysis, which examines the firm's strengths, weaknesses, opportunities and threats.

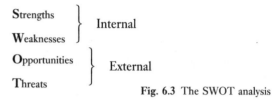

Strengths

Weaknesses

} Internal

Opportunities

Threats

} External

Fig. 6.3 The SWOT analysis

Method of analysis

The best way to tackle a SWOT analysis is to involve as many people as possible from within your company who have responsibility for marketing or contact with customers. If you do not have a marketing expert within your company, you should consider involving an outside consultant (perhaps with the aid of a DTI or Training Agency grant), to lead these sessions. You should sit round the table and start by getting the participants to write their own list of what they feel are the firm's strengths. Around fifteen minutes should be allowed for this so that everyone can make their list as comprehensive as possible. Participants should not communicate with each other at this stage. When everyone has finished writing, the session leader asks everyone in turn to read out and explain their points, writing them on a flip chart as they are mentioned. After the first person's list, only new strengths will be listed. Although discussion should be encouraged in order to clarify the exact nature of strengths mentioned, there should be no criticism at this stage. The objective is to produce a fully comprehensive listing of the company's strengths.

At the end of it you should have a long list. To be of value, the strengths now need to be qualified with a view to arriving at the firm's key strengths. The best way of doing this is to ask each person round the table to look at the master list and write down what they see as the firm's five key strengths. The session leader then writes these on the flipchart. This usually results in a new list which will probably contain more than five strengths, but one which is now reasonably manageable.

The next step is to agree on how strong each strength really is, usually by getting all the participants to agree on a mark out of ten for each strength. This grading will identify those things the firm is best at.

There is one final step which needs to be taken. Identifying the firm's strongest attributes is important but it is not necessarily the case that these are solely responsible for the firm's marketing success. For example, you may be very proud of the fact that you offer a next day repair and maintenance service to all owners of your equipment, and, because you never fail to honour this pledge, the group may award it a mark of 10 out 10 as a key strength. However, if a competing firm offers a same day service pledge, your own key strength now begins to look a little less attractive. Strengths of course, are all relative. You must therefore try to look at your own strengths through the eyes of customers who will compare your strengths with those of your competitors. Your real strengths are those where you most outperform the competition. As a result of this comparison exercise, you may need to modify the marks you had given to your key strengths.

You can do this exercise alone, but a group of people, however small, will almost always do it better because an idea from one person sparks off a thought from another. If you have only a few employees you should involve everyone who has any contact with customers. If you have no suitable employees, try to arrange a session with an outsider such as a friend, relative or business associate who knows your business very well.

Internal analysis

The firm's strengths and weaknesses should be seen, quite simply, as things which the firm is good at, and things that it is bad at. These strengths and weaknesses are internal, they are under your control. You can therefore plan to build on your strengths and to reduce or eliminate your weaknesses. Using group sessions you should identify your key strengths and weaknesses in relation to your competitors. Any internal factors which have a beneficial or adverse effect on your firm's success in the marketplace should therefore be highlighted. Factors such as products, people, resources, cost structure, the firm's prominence and image in the marketplace, the extent of its distribution coverage, and its premises and location could all be seen as a strength or a weakness.

Prince Components: strengths and weaknesses recognized by the company's internal analysis

Strengths

1 Products built precisely to the customer's specification.
2 Wide range of different models available.
3 Virtually any enquiry for the component can be met.
4 Company seldom refuses a customer request.
5 Company specializes in the manufacture of the component.
6 Large share of the market for the product.
7 High quality standards.
8 Excellent quality documentation.
9 Ability to work to recognized UK design codes.
10 Spare capacity improves responsiveness.
11 Some flexibility on delivery times for urgent orders.
12 Good site, with all manufacturing operations in-house.
13 Good internal communications.
14 Quick decision making.
15 Good working conditions, good labour relations.

16 Up-to-date technology, including CNC lathes, and a computer used for design, costing, accounts, and sales records purposes.
17 Strong research and development activity.
18 Strong in-house technical expertise.
19 Image of technical competence.
20 Firm used by customers as source of technical advice.
21 Good telephone relations with customers.
22 Very impressive customer list.
23 Very good after-sales service.
24 Financially very strong.
25 New patented product.
26 Range of materials used in manufacture.
27 Good stands at the two main industry exhibitions.

Weaknesses
1 Inadequate knowledge of markets and customers.
2 Very few visits made to customers.
3 Virtually no selling effort.
4 Insufficient advertising and PR.
5 Leads from exhibitions, or elsewhere, rarely followed up.
6 Out-of-date literature.
7 Some products not covered by literature.
8 Neglect of export markets.
9 Little after-sale follow-up (unless requested).
10 Response time on quotations could be better.
11 No follow-up of quotations.
12 Long delivery times.
13 Delivery times are not always met.
14 High overheads.
15 High prices.

External analysis

Outside your firm will be a whole range of factors that you have no control over. You can only attempt to steer your company towards opportunities and away from threats in the external environment. Items to be included in the external analysis include the environmental and marketplace factors discussed in Chapter 2, such as political, economic, social and technological trends; market size and growth; the number and strength of competitors; and sources of supply.

As with the internal analysis, you should rank the external factors in order of importance. As far as opportunities are concerned, such a grading can be estimated in two ways. Firstly, the absolute extent of all opportunities should be evaluated. Some market opportunities will be huge, with market sizes of millions of pounds and strong growth, other opportunities will be identified in much smaller specialized markets. The second step is to evaluate the relevance of each opportunity to your company bearing in mind your strengths and weaknesses identified in your internal analysis. For example, a small niche market, ideally suited to your key strengths, in which you could aim for market leadership, may represent a much greater opportunity to your company than a huge growth market which will be aggressively pursued by large companies.

The evaluation of threats is also a two stage process. Firstly, the gravity of the threat should be considered. How serious to the prosperity, or even the existence of your firm, would each threat be if it was realized? Secondly, you must assess the likelihood of the occurrence of each threat. For example, new legislation banning the sale of fresh eggs due to a salmonella threat would be devastating for chicken farmers but the likelihood of its occurrence is very low. On the other hand, the threat of a small reduction in demand for fresh eggs because of a health scare would have an adverse effect on egg producers, albeit only a slight one, but, because the likelihood of this occurrence is much greater, it would be seen as the more significant of the two threats facing chicken farmers.

Prince Components: opportunities and threats recognized by the company's external analysis

Opportunities
1 Overseas markets in English-speaking countries worldwide.
2 Large OEMs (original equipment manufacturers) in France and Germany.
3 Buoyancy of the UK motor industry, particularly the growth of Japanese manufacturing plants.
4 The Single European Market, 1992.
5 Water industry privatization.
6 Pending legislation on pollution.
7 Potential new applications in food processing plant.
8 Potential new applications in chemical processing plant.
9 Potential new applications in the pharmaceutical industry.
10 Service and spares market with existing users.
11 Greater use of distributors to broaden UK coverage.
12 New materials.

Threats
1 Competitors.
2 Dependence on the oil market, which will be declining in the North Sea.
3 Water privatization – the French threat.
4 Exchange rate fluctuations.
5 Low cost competing products.
6 BS 5750, particularly if one of the major competitors is first to gain approval.
7 1992, particularly the threat of German technical standards being embraced by the industry.
8 OEMs' technological advances, which may reduce or even eliminate the need for the company's components.
9 Shortage of skilled labour.
10 Poaching of key staff.

The matching process

An ideal way of identifying those areas of opportunity which most closely match the strengths of the company is to write a very concise summary of the whole SWOT analysis.

Prince Components: summary of key SWOTs

Strengths

1 Technical leaders in the firm's narrow product field.
2 Totally flexible response to customer requests for products, service and advice.
3 High quality of manufacture, materials, documentation and design.

Weaknesses

1 Neglect of sales and marketing activities.
2 Delivery times.
3 High prices.

Opportunities

1 New industry applications, especially food processing.
2 Export markets in Europe.
3 Water privatization.

Threats

1 Overdependence on the offshore oil market.
2 French competition (1992 and water privatization).
3 Competitor(s), particularly if BS 5750 approval gained.

Positioning statement

At this point, it can be very useful to compile the SWOT summary into a brief positioning statement which clearly defines the company's position in relation to its competitors and in relation to the opportunities which it faces.

Prince Components: positioning statement

'From the point of view of product quality and technical expertise, Prince Components is the leading firm in a very specialized market. However, lack of marketing skills have led to an underexploitation of these strengths and to overdependence on certain market segments where the firm enjoys good personal relations with regular customers. New opportunities will be afforded by the events surrounding 1992 and water privatization and there are additional opportunities for new applications of the product. Threats may arise from more aggressive competitors, from the UK, France or Germany whose superior marketing expertise may enable them to corner attractive segments of the market.'

The time for marketing research

The best starting point for market research is through the knowledge and experience of your own staff, using the SWOT analysis as a framework, and conveyed at a group session(s). Having done this you should have a fair idea of the firm's current position in the marketplace.

However, the analysis resulting from the group sessions is entirely subjective, based only upon the knowledge and beliefs of the participants around the table. Market research techniques should therefore be employed at this stage to check the accuracy of the firm's SWOT analysis. Unless the views of customers are canvassed, the validity of the firm's internal analysis can not be checked. Equally, it would be wise to check the firm's view of opportunities and threats against objective sources of external information.

Using market research at this stage of the planning process does not necessarily mean the commissioning of a costly survey. A good method of checking the firm's SWOT analysis can be for each member of your planning group to devote one or two days to interviewing customers (or other relevant industry experts), in person or by telephone. An agreed series of questions can be asked, the results reported back to the group, and the SWOT findings reappraised in the light of the information which emerges from the exercise.

Objectives

Objectives answer the question 'where do we want to be?'

Marketing objectives must be precise

As shown in the diagram opposite, there are three important rules when setting marketing objectives. They should be relevant, which means compatible with your firm's SWOT analysis. They should be achievable: unrealistic targets can do more harm than good, since they often act as demotivators to the staff concerned who cannot see any point in making any effort trying to achieve the unachievable. Thirdly, and most importantly, objectives should be measurable. An objective is pointless if you cannot identify unambiguously whether or not it has been achieved. Measurable objectives also enable you to monitor your progress towards their attainment on an ongoing basis. This continuous monitoring and control of the marketing plan's implementation is usually fundamental to its success.

Formulating your marketing objectives

Developing and wording your own marketing objectives can be a difficult task. It will be examined in relation to Prince Components, shown on the next few pages.

The starting point must be your financial goals. They translate easily into sales targets, which must be split into annual turnover objectives. If you wish to accelerate your firm's growth rate it would be wise to reflect this fact through a staged increase in turnover growth, as shown in objective 1. Your profit objectives must also be reflected in the marketing objectives because of their implications for pricing. This is shown in objective 2. If you are to maintain long-term growth you will need to innovate on a continuous basis. Marketing objectives should lay down clear goals in this respect, as shown in objective 3. Finally, since professional marketing is essential if you have ambitious growth targets, you should set specific goals for improving your firm's marketing as shown in objective 4.

Prince Components: marketing objectives

1 To double sales over a three year period from £3 million to £6 million. This will involve annual sales increases as follows:
Year 1:   20 per cent increase to: £3,600,000
Year 2:   25 per cent increase to: £4,500,000
Year 3:   33 per cent increase to: £6,000,000

2 To maintain their profit margins at the existing level. The firm's overall net return on sales should not, therefore, fall below 15 per cent so pricing policies must ensure the maintenance of adequate average margins. If

Good objectives should be:

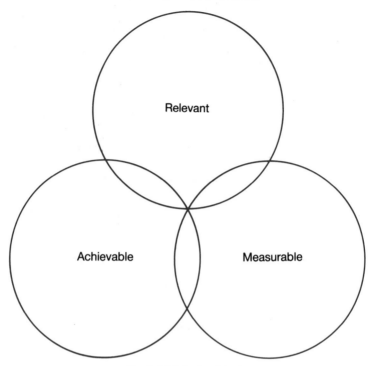

Fig. 6.4 Marketing objectives

returns from some product lines sold in certain market segments are projected to fall below 15 per cent the shortfall on profits must be compensated for by higher returns in other segments.

3 The firm will continue its policy of investing 3 per cent of projected sales revenue in research and development activities with the objective of introducing three major new products during the three year period. Specifically, these should include:

 a the replacement for product B by month nine, year one
 b the new product for the motor industry by month three, year two
 c the new product for the oil and gas industry by month three, year three

4 A key objective for the company during the three year period is to develop its marketing capability. To this end the following specific objectives should be achieved by the end of the period:

 a the implementation of a computerized marketing control system to:
    record details of customers and prospects
    record details of marketing expenses
    monitor response to marketing activities
    monitor salesforce performance
 b the improvement of responsiveness to customers such that by the end of year one a response is made to all enquiries from whatever source within 24 hours

c the specification of a marketing information system by month three, year
one, and its implementation by month six; the system to cover the whole
European Community

d at least one employee to have a good working knowledge of German,
French and Spanish by the end of the three year planning cycle

Strategy

Strategy in business is about allocating resources and deploying them in
such a way as to maximize your advantages over the competition.
Marketing strategy can be defined as:

'What products to what markets?'

It is useful to have a framework to guide the development of your
marketing strategy. An ideal framework is shown in fig. 6.5.

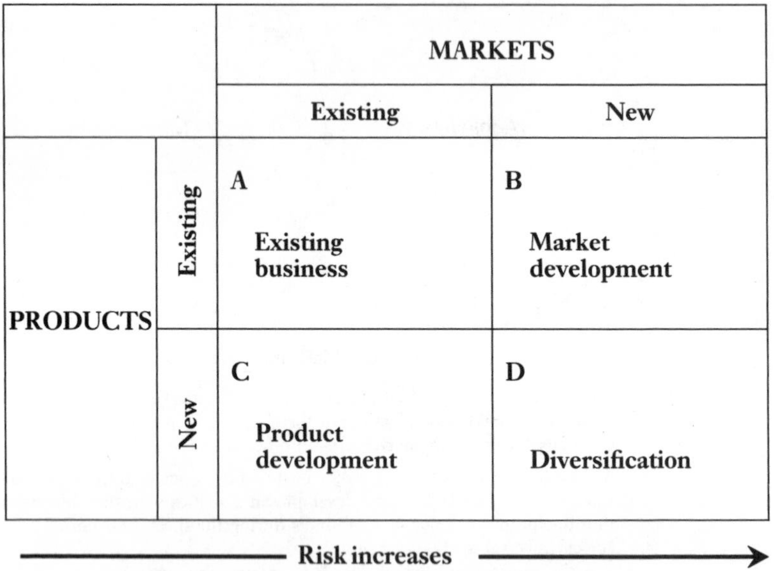

		MARKETS	
		Existing	New
PRODUCTS	Existing	**A** Existing business	**B** Market development
	New	**C** Product development	**D** Diversification

Risk increases →

Risk increases →

Fig. 6.5 What products shall we sell to what markets?

The achievement of your marketing objectives must involve the sale of
certain products to certain markets. Your marketing strategy should specify
exactly which products you need to sell to which market segments in order
to achieve your objectives. Referring to fig. 6.5 it is usually most practical
to start with the box which is closest to your existing position, and,
referring in turn to each of the four boxes, list the product-market areas
where you aim to make sales.

Existing business

In the first year of a marketing strategy you would anticipate the bulk of
sales coming from existing products sold to existing markets. Since this is

the easiest and least risky business to pursue, you should turn your thoughts initially to specifying all your existing product-market areas and estimating their growth over the next three years. Increased sales may result from growth in the markets concerned or it may result from your aggressive marketing which will improve your competitiveness. For comparison purposes it is useful to include sales figures for the year immediately preceding the first year of your plan.

Prince Components: development of their existing business

	Years				
	0	**1**	**2**	**3**	
Product A to oil and gas, UK	1.2m	1.3m	1.3m	1.3m	*Number of sales*
Product A to chemical industry	.5m	.6m	.8m	1.2m	
Product A to printing industry	.2m	.3m	.4m	.6m	
Product A to European agents	.5m	.6m	.8m	1.0m	
Product B to motor industry	.6m	.5m	.3m	0	

Market development

This strategy, which means selling existing products to new markets, involves finding new users or, possibly, new uses for your products or services. This can involve geographic expansion or moving into new market segments. Potential opportunities for these moves should have been identified at the SWOT analysis stage.

Prince Components: market development strategy

In the first year it will be difficult to penetrate new markets but it is essential that a start be made. Prince Components' SWOT analysis identified the food processing and water industries as the most promising opportunities, so if they are to be successfully exploited, a start must be made in Year 1. In the longer term the pharmaceutical industry, more distant overseas markets and the European OEMs could be tackled. However, it is important to accept that sales take time to build up in new markets, as reflected in the figures below.

	Years				
	0	**1**	**2**	**3**	
Product A to food processing	0	.1m	.2m	.3m	*Number of sales*
Product A to water industry	0	.1m	.1m	.2m	
Product A to pharmaceutical	0	0	.1m	.2m	
Product A to North American agents	0	0	0	.1m	

Product development

From a marketing point of view, introducing new products to existing markets, particularly when they are replacements for existing products, holds less uncertainty than attempting to penetrate new markets where the company is unknown. However, getting new products to a position where they can be promoted to customers is not a straightforward task. New product development is covered in Chapter 7.

Prince Components: product development strategy

It is the objective of the company to introduce three new products during the three year period covered by the strategic plan. Sales for the replacement product can be expected to climb quite rapidly because the plan only really shows the product taking over the existing sales of the original Product B. Sales for totally new products can not usually be expected to take off quickly unless the firm operates in very fast changing markets.

		Years			
	0	1	2	3	
Product B2 to motor industry	0	.1m	.3m	.6m	*Number of sales*
Product C to motor industry	0	0	.1m	.2m	
Product D to oil and gas industry	0	0	.0	.1m	

Diversification

Prince Components plans to achieve its sales objectives without diversifying. For most small companies this is a wise strategy. The further you move away from your existing business, the more risk you are taking and the more unpredictable your projections become. However, through a series of small product developments and small market developments you can gradually diversify over a period of years. It is vital to avoid the huge risk involved in jumping straight into a totally new market with a new product.

Tactics

Tactical plans involve a series of action points which will guide the implementation of your marketing strategy. Selecting the right products to sell to the right markets will be fundamental to your firm's success but a sound strategy can easily be sabotaged by poor implementation.

Product

Assuming the firm will have quarterly review periods, tactical plans should cover the next three months in great detail, with salient actions itemized for the following nine months. New product development schedules will be very important as failure to meet deadlines in this area could jeopardize the entire marketing effort. New packaging may be required, which may involve action plans covering the selection of an outside design consultant, the approval of final designs, consultations with photographers, printers and packaging manufacturers to produce the new packaging and test on its durability. New packaging may not sound like an enormous task, but the successful coordination of many different activities will be required if the task is to be completed to schedule.

Place

Place is all about those aspects of your marketing programme which improve the availability and accessibility of your product. Let's say that your marketing plans have shown that if you wanted to expand, you would need to appoint agents in two additional European countries. Once again, it is a task which will demand that many detailed action points are implemented to schedule. For example, it may be necessary to approach facilitators such as the British Overseas Trade Board, (found at your regional DTI office), your bank or the London embassy of the country concerned. You may think it worthwhile visiting one of the libraries mentioned in Chapter 5, and you may have contacts in the UK who already trade in the overseas market whose advice should be sought. Having identified a number of potential agents in the two countries concerned you may wish to visit them to select the most suitable agent for each country and, having made your choice you would be advised to check out their credentials via the BOTB's Overseas Status Report Service. It should be clear that such a multiplicity of tasks will not be performed according to plan unless a precise schedule of events is worked out and adhered to.

Price

Price levels can be difficult to determine. Detailed costings will be needed, information on the pricing of competing products will have to be sought, the requirements of distributors ascertained and the views of potential customers canvassed before the firm can decide on a pricing policy. Having determined the prices and discount structures, price lists will have to be designed, printed and distributed. Some products may need the price displayed on the packaging, which will add a further requirement to the scheduling. Further details about pricing are given in Chapter 9.

Promotion

Promotional tasks can vary widely (see Chapters 10 and 11) but most require a significant level of detailed planning if they are to be implemented successfully. Consider the task of sending out a press release to accompany the launch of a new product. Relevant media such as trade journals, local press and perhaps local radio and TV need to be identified through publications such as *BRAD* or *Benn's Media Directory*, and addresses and contact names noted. The text for the press release must be prepared and printed, with as many as one hundred copies often being released. Photographs always improve a press release but will require the booking of a good professional photographer, the selection of suitable photos and the printing of the correct number. Media will often have long deadlines, so some press releases will have to be sent out well ahead of time if publicity is to coincide with the launch.

The action plan

Once you have completed your tactical planning, it is essential to specify the precise actions which must be taken by named individuals at particular times. This 'who does what when' action plan is best displayed in the form of a spreadsheet, showing weeks across the top and actions, (with the person responsible), down the side (see fig. 6.6). Detailed action plans should cover a three month period.

Component A Action Plan

Activity	Week commencing									
	8/1/90	15/1/90	22/1/90	29/1/90	5/2/90	12/2/90	19/2/90	26/2/90	5/3/90	12/3/90
Compile mailing list (GC)	●									
Design mailshot card (AD)	●									
Seek printing quotes (GC)	●									
Print mailshot card (GC)			●							
Send mailshot wave 1 (GC)				●						
Send mailshot wave 2 (GC)					●					
Send mailshot wave 3 (GC)						●				
Telephone follow-up wave 1 (GC)					●					
Telephone follow-up wave 2 (GC)						●				
Telephone follow-up wave 3 (GC)							●			
Design product leaflet (AD)		●								
Arrange photographer (AD)		●								
Photographs back (AD)			●							
Write text for leaflets (AD)			●							
Arrange printer (AD)			●							
Leaflets back from printer (AD)					●					
Write data sheets (AD)				●						
Type data sheets (MJ)					●					
Photocopy data sheets (MJ)					●					
Write press release (AD)					●					
Compile journal addresses (GC)				●						
Type press release (MJ)						●				
Photocopy press release (MJ)						●				
Send out press release (GC)							●			

Fig. 6.6 Action plan spreadsheet

As you can see, the action plan should be very detailed, covering all the actions, however small, that need to be carried out if the marketing plan is to be implemented efficiently. You will find that such a clear action plan will help everyone concerned to organize their time and it will ensure that nothing gets overlooked.

Control and evaluation

The detailed action plan will also help the firm to monitor the implementation of its marketing plan. It is recommended that formal review meetings are held every three months to discuss progress during the previous quarter and plan ahead for the next quarter, including writing the next detailed action plan. If you have a great deal of marketing activity taking place, less formal monthly progress meetings will also be necessary. Review meetings should evaluate whether the firm is still on course to achieve its marketing objectives. If not, an explanation must be found. For example, if there is too much work for the existing staff to cope with, someone else must be recruited or the plans must be phased over a longer period of time. Maybe an unavoidable problem such as a mail strike caused a delay. Sometimes, sales are lower than expected. In this case you must decide whether the firm itself is to blame or whether demand in the marketplace is less than expected. If the fault lies within the firm, measures must be taken to overcome it, but if it lies outside the firm, the marketing plan will have to be amended, since there is no point striving to achieve impossible sales targets. Review meetings should be attended by everyone who has any involvement in the firm's sales and marketing work. Participation in decision making is a very important factor in ensuring everybody's commitment to the implementation of the marketing plan.

Summary

1 Planning is essential to the success of the small business and can be carried out in a very straightforward way.

2 A thorough SWOT analysis, reinforced by appropriate marketing research, is fundamental to the development of a good marketing plan.

3 Precise marketing objectives are very important. Unless your objectives are explicit and measurable you will never know whether or not you have achieved them.

4 To achieve your objectives you will need to develop a marketing strategy, specifying which products you will sell to which markets.

5 Tactical plans are about the short-term implementation of your marketing strategy and should be written in the form of a clear action plan which specifies who does what and when.

6 Regular review meetings should be held to monitor the implementation of the marketing plan and take corrective action if necessary.

Action

1 Carry out a SWOT analysis for your company and summarize the key factors (three for each group).

2 What are your marketing objectives?

3 Explain how you will achieve those objectives through:
a existing business
b market development
c product development

7 Products

Aims of this chapter

This chapter is about managing your products or services. There are no fundamental differences between the marketing of products and the marketing of services: both should be seen in terms of the benefits they offer to customers. This section will examine:

- The need to innovate
- Competitive edge through added value
- The importance of branding
- Special aspects of service marketing

The need to innovate

Product life cycles

All products have a finite life and pass through a life cycle which is similar to human development: from birth, through growth, to maturity, on to decline and, eventually, death.

The length of profitable life and the duration of each stage will vary significantly according to the product involved. Some commodity products appear to have an almost indefinite mature stage whereas other products, such as information technology products, show rapid growth, short

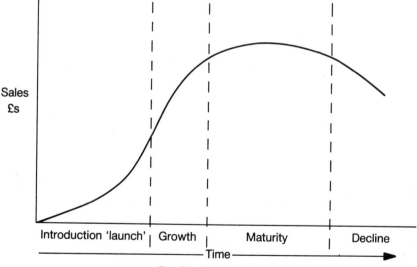

Fig. 7.1 The product life cycle

maturity and sharp decline. However, the main purpose of the product life cycle diagram is to show that no products have an indefinite life which means that innovation strategies are essential to business survival and growth.

A basket of products

Some firms run into problems because thay have too many products at the decline stage in their life cycle. Once in that position, it can be very difficult to suddenly come up with new products to fill the gap. Therefore, you must have a plan which ensures that you never end up in this situation.

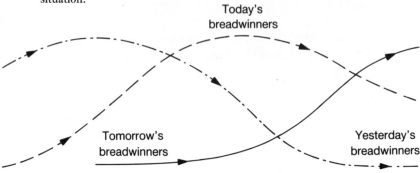

Today's
breadwinners

Tomorrow's
breadwinners

Yesterday's
breadwinners

Fig. 7.2 A well balanced range of products

1 **Today's breadwinners**. 'Today's breadwinners' are at their most profitable life cycle stage, the mature stage, so they make lots of money. Their development costs have been covered, they are likely to be well known in the market and the company is experienced and efficient in their manufacture. However, remember that their popularity will not last for ever.

2 **Yesterday's breadwinners**. Sooner or later all products become 'yesterday's breadwinners', it can happen suddenly and unexpectedly. It is therefore vital that when this happens you should have new products ready to take their place.

3 **Tomorrow's breadwinners**. 'Tomorrow's breadwinners' can be very time-consuming and costly to develop, so you must have a policy of using part of the profit generated by 'today's breadwinners' to fund the development of the new products to ensure the survival and growth of your company. Innovation should be seen as a continuous programme, vital to the continued health of any business, and not simply as an activity which will be pursued when necessary. By the time you have identified the need for a new product it will almost certainly be too late to begin the development process.

Developing new products

At this stage, it is worth pointing out that a new product does not have to be completely 'new' – it can be a variation on an existing product, for example, perhaps a new flavour or a new size. So bear this in mind when considering your plans for new products.

The steps involved in developing new products are shown in fig. 7.3. Steps 1 and 2 are covered thoroughly in the second chapter of the companion volume *Starting a Small Business*, the rest in other chapters of this book.

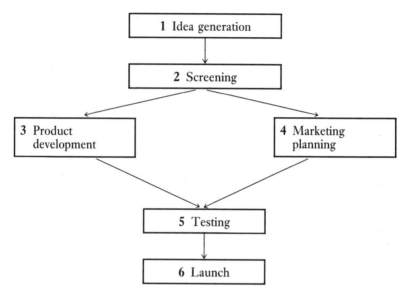

Fig. 7.3 Steps in the new product development process

Most new products fail. Although there are no universally accepted figures, some authorities suggest that over 90 per cent of new product ideas fail, either before they reach the market or soon after their launch. The main reason for so many failures is that companies rush into new projects, often on the basis of hunches. The best way to avoid failure is to be thorough about all the steps shown in fig. 7.3 and to follow these basic rules:

Rule 1: Never throw good money after bad. It's common sense, but many firms do it because they get emotionally carried away with new projects. It is more sensible to view your new projects with suspicion, as a snowball, rolling downhill, getting bigger and bigger (i.e. costlier and costlier) as it goes and continuously increasing its momentum (i.e. becoming ever more difficult to stop). As a manager, you must remain in control of this snowball. As it rolls along you must constantly check that it's still a good idea. If a project needs to be terminated, the closer to the beginning of its life that you can make the decision, the less costly it will be. However, it is never too late to abort a questionable project, because if you carry on 'throwing good money after bad', you will only be increasing your losses.

Rule 2: Consult customers. At the screening stage, before any real development work has begun, it is vital to discuss your idea with as many knowledgeable people as possible. Their objective appraisals may be a more accurate reflection of likely reaction of the market than your enthusiasm. At the product development stage, technical people should be forced to break all their instincts to beaver away in secret. Most new products do not need to be kept secret and there is more to be gained from discussing their development with potential customers than there is from keeping them secret. The same principle applies at the testing stage. Many small firms do not have the facilities to test products as rigorously as they will be tested in real use. The best way to test them is with the cooperation of a small number of friendly customers who will agree to test them in full working use.

Rule 3: Make sure there is a market. Market research must begin very early in the new product development process, looking at broad issues such as market size and likely competitors. It's no use continuing with the project if the evidence suggests that potential sales are not very promising. As the product development process continues, so the research should become more specific, using customers' views to guide this process. The testing stage should ideally involve a very limited product launch to a restricted test market to ensure that real customers will pay real money for the new product before the firm is committed to a full-scale launch. Launching the product is often more expensive than all the other stages put together as you have to tool up for production, and maybe employ extra staff. Promoting a new product will often take a big chunk of that year's promotional budget. Most serious of all, you will be committed. If it flops you will be saddled with a damaged reputation as well as with products you can't sell. So even at the pre-launch stage it can still be in your financial interests to stop rather than carry on.

Rule 4: If you have a good idea, protect it. Many small firms lose control of good ideas because of a lack of understanding of the patenting process. It isn't cheap, but the sums of money involved are small compared to the future profits that you could lose from a good invention.

Protecting new products

The way to protect new products from competitors is not to be secretive to the point of turning into a recluse, but to use the full power of the legal protection which is open to you. However, it is useful to consider some of the potential pitfalls in this process.

1 **Patents.** The most powerful form of protection is a patent, which provides a twenty year monopoly, but costs around £1500 for the UK alone, and another £1000 for each additional country in which you require protection. Although there have been attempts to make patents more widely applicable, the UK and the USA have so far remained outside all such international agreements. The most important single aspect of the patenting process is that you must make your initial application *before* you

have disclosed your ideas to anyone else, even friends. You then have a one year period in which to file applications in additional countries. The patenting process can thus take a considerable time, but once you have filed your application you are free to consult with customers, and if necessary you can modify the details of your application.

2 Registered design. There are cheaper and simpler alternatives to patents. If your new product has a distinctive visual appearance it may be feasible to register the design, which can be done for little more than £100, but could open the way for someone to copy the product if they can make the external appearance sufficiently different.

3 Registered trademarks. For high volume, low cost products, a registered trademark may be the most cost-effective solution. The trademark does not prevent copying of the core product, but it is often the additional things associated with the core product, name, for example, which are most highly valued by customers. In such cases, the trademark can protect the bulk of your marketing advantages.

4 Copyright. For potential new products which do not have a tangible design or external appearance, such as ideas or, perhaps, a computer programme, the law of copyright can offer the most useful form of protection. The key here is your ability to prove that you had the idea first, which involves the keeping of thorough and tamper proof recording systems showing who developed what and when. Bound notebooks with dated pages, initialled regularly by more than one person, will help. External validation of dates on documents such as a post office or bank date stamp would increase their authority.

5 Further help. If you have doubts about legal protection it is essential to seek professional advice. If you are a member of a trade association or a chamber of commerce, help may be available from one of these sources. Alternatively, you can approach the Institute of Inventors who will assist in finding out whether ideas are new (and therefore protectable), whether they will work and whether they are commercially viable. For further details contact:

The Institute of Inventors, 19–32 Fosse Way, Ealing, London W13 0BZ. Tel: 01 998 3540.

Adding value

One of the chief roles of marketing is to add value to whatever goods or services the firm sells. Some products are highly technical, innovative and possibly covered by patent. Such products are clearly differentiated from competing products and will often command a premium price. However, the core products of most firms are less easily distinguishable from those offered by the competition. The more value in the form of extras that comes with the product, the more it is likely to hold off competition.

The diagram overleaf should be seen as a guide, not a prescription. Few firms will offer all the extras listed. The extras you should offer are the ones which add most value in the eyes of your customers. Find out what they value by asking them.

Fig. 7.4 Adding value

1 **Quality.** Everybody values quality, but some firms are now adding to the quality of their products in the eyes of customers by gaining approval to BS 5750. This British Standard is a badge of quality. Government grants for quality assurance are available under the Enterprise Initiative scheme – contact your local DTI office for details.

2 **Design.** Many products, particularly in industrial markets, are of very plain design. Good, modern design is not only attractive, it can make your products different, and therefore more easily remembered. However, design does not just mean product design, it could include things like premises (e.g. a restaurant), signs and logos, and packaging. The Enterprise Initiative offers small firms help with design.

3 **Packaging.** Packaging performs two functions: protection and promotion.

a Protection. Its protective function is crucial, and applies to most products. Inadequate packaging means that parcels and cartons can arrive in a very tatty state, which is bad for your image even if the goods inside remain undamaged. Don't take short cuts on the packaging: stronger packaging is a lot cheaper than replacing damaged products.

b Promotion. In the self-service environment, products have to speak for themselves and sometimes customers will select the brand which shouts the loudest – the one which is most visible on the shelf. Since you will usually have no control over the shelf location of your product, and it could be tucked away in a rather inaccessible spot, there are two things which your packaging must achieve:

Impact. It must stand out but it must also convey the right message. It's no good having a weird and wonderful pack design which attracts attention but does not spell out what is inside the packaging.

Find-time. You want your packaging to minimize the amount of time it takes to find it on the shelf. This means making it memorable and not changing it too often. Changing your packaging is as risky as changing your address and should only be done if there is evidence that your existing packaging is performing poorly.

4 Guarantees. There is plenty of evidence that the 'Marks and Spencer' type money back guarantee is very cost-effective in the long run. It gives customers confidence, so you win and keep more customers. If your product is not good enough to guarantee you should not be selling it. If the product is good enough the more reservations customers might have about doing business with you, the more important a clear guarantee statement is. If they don't know your company or are not familiar with your product, guarantees are crucial. It is not even a particularly costly process. Even guarantees which promise a full refund if the customer is not totally satisfied after 14 days usually have an extremely low redemption rate.

5 Delivery. Most customers value reliable delivery more than quick delivery. However, if you can offer it reliably, a super-quick delivery or service can give you a competitive edge in the marketplace.

6 Service. Many firms maintain a competitive edge in the marketplace through offering good service. This can mean little more than being very polite and looking after the customers' needs. If they want technical details or special quotes, provide them as quickly as possible and with good grace – it's amazing how many firms do not. If a customer has problems after he has purchased, make it your *top priority* to solve them. Market research surveys show that many companies are still very poor on service, and that customers recognize the good ones and the bad ones. Offering good service is the best way to keep existing customers and is much cheaper than winning new ones.

7 Credit. Although offering credit does add value for the customer, it can be a dangerous route to follow for you and your small business.

8 Image. The total offering of your product, its quality, packaging, design, together with the level of service provided by your company, will give you an 'image' in customers minds. You do not create an image through advertising, you earn it by the way you behave in the marketplace. A good image is built over the years, a bad one can be gained in a single day. All the points made in this chapter contribute to your image. You cannot afford to neglect any of them.

Austin Trumanns Steel:
adding value

Operating at the most competitive end of the steel stockholding market, Austin Trumanns Steel supplies general steels from four distribution centres.

It was during a regular planning meeting that the idea of a delivery guarantee arose. All stockholders tend to promote their delivery service, but Austin Trumanns suspected that little more than lip service was paid by some of their competitors to living up to those promises, whereas they knew that their own delivery record was very good. Therefore, why not match their own strength with a market opportunity and offer a delivery guarantee?

The concept is simple. When placing an order, customers usually specify a delivery date. If Austin Trumanns accept the proposed delivery date, and the customer requests 'Touchdown Guarantee' (the brand name given by the firm to the scheme), the company has to deliver on time or pay the customer a self-imposed fine. This is payable in the form of a credit note worth 10 per cent of the invoice value of each item not delivered. This has helped Austin Trumanns to win new customers. It has also enabled the company to focus its attention on its own efficiency and service levels. Because the guarantee scheme demanded the implementation of new, fully documented operating procedures, when the company does fail to get delivery on time these new procedures can identify where it went wrong, thus helping to ensure that good practice is maintained and failures minimized.

The 'Touchdown Guarantee' has thus added value to a product, which wins new customers and fosters the goodwill of existing ones.

Fig. 7.5 The inside pages of Austin Trumanns folded A5 leaflet, giving details of the 'Touchdown Guarantee' scheme

Branding

A brand, quite simply, is a product with an identity. Without branding, a product is like a faceless person with no personality. Anything can be branded and should be branded, whether destined for industrial or consumer markets. A brand image projects all that is good about your products, and should encompass the following features.

1 **Brand name.** Few entrepreneurs should need reminding about the importance of names. Consumers are surrounded by powerful brand names which constantly influence their purchases, either through favourable associations or through their greater familiarity and prominence in the marketplace. Yet, despite this constant evidence of the power of brand names, many products go unnamed and many businesses are saddled with meaningless and forgettable names.

Brand names and business names should conform to the following criteria:

a they should be short
b they should be easy to read
c they should be easy to pronounce
d they should describe the product, or the company's activities
e they should communicate a benefit

Prontaprint, Happy Eater and Kwik-Fit are good examples.

2 **Logo.** A clear logo can reinforce the brand name by enhancing its visual appeal. The key here is clarity. Anything which makes the name more difficult to read should be ruled out. The logo should be striking but simple. It is better to be without a logo than to have one which is too complex. Slogans fall into a similar category. If they are complementary to the brand name and communicate additional benefits, they can be helpful, but long, complicated or cryptic slogans should not be considered by most small firms.

3 **Brand identity.** The brand identity is the image which you wish your brand to have. Many buyers will form a relatively simple notion of your product in their own minds. A strong brand identity will help customers to form the right image of your product. To achieve a clear brand image you must identify the key aspects of your product (and its value added services) which give it a competitive edge in the marketplace. You must then take every opportunity to promote these benefits. Through the consistent communication of a small number of clear benefits, the right brand identity will develop.

4 **Packaging and brochures.** Packaging, brochures, mailshots, in fact anything you have printed, offer an ideal opportunity to reinforce brand name, logo and identity. You should brand constantly on all such printed materials. The more times people see it the more they will remember it.

5 **Consistency.** In the long run the chief factor in the development of a strong brand image will be consistency. There are two aspects to consistency. Firstly, trappings of branding such as the name, logo, slogan and packaging should not be tampered with. The most successful

consumer brands have been very consistent in this respect. Secondly, the actual product should measure up to its image. If customers are ever disappointed with the real benefits of the product (compared to their expectations), the brand image will suffer. A poor reputation can be easily gained but is very hard to overcome.

Marketing services

The fundamental principles of marketing apply equally to both services and tangible products. However, there are a number of characteristics of services which may demand making slight modifications to your marketing approach.

Intangibility

Unlike goods, services cannot be seen, touched, smelt, tasted or tried on for size, all of which can make them more difficult to buy. For example, if you are choosing between two sofas there will be some visible differences which make comparison easier. If you are choosing between two pension schemes, the means of comparing one with the other may be much less obvious. Thus, whereas the seller of goods was advised earlier in this chapter to augment his product with value added services, the seller of services would be well advised to try and surround his product with tangible symbols that the customer can easily relate to. For example, estate agents' services are usually associated with tangibles such as professional sales literature, eye catching 'For Sale' boards and smart offices full of glossy photographs of houses.

The way in which successful estate agents manage their image to emphasize the tangible benefits can serve as an example to all service marketers. You must make maximum advantage of all the image building tangible features which are involved in the provision of your service. These may include:

a your premises
b the people providing the service
c the equipment used in the performance of the service
d the clothing worn by the staff providing the service
e vehicles
f stationery, order forms and company literature

All of these things help customers form images of your product. They should therefore present a clear image, and they should exploit every opportunity to brand the service. Always give your service a brand name. It may become the most tangible feature that people can relate to.

Inseparability

The production and consumption of many services are inseparable. To take advantage of a bus service, for example, both you and the bus must make the journey at the same time. If you have your hair cut you have to be sitting there at the same time as the hairdresser is working. Buyers of most physical goods see only the finished product, neatly packaged, with all the blemishes ironed out. They do not stand in the factory observing every step in its manufacture. The buyers of many services do.

The key implication of this is that your staff will have a huge effect on the level of customer satisfaction. Careful selection of staff and thorough training is necessary to ensure that your staff display professional competence, courtesy, intelligence, friendliness and any other attributes which may contribute to this satisfaction.

Perishability

You cannot find a tangible product which is more perishable than a seat on a bus or an overnight stay in a hotel. Since production and consumption are simultaneous, services are instantly perishable if they have not been bought by the time of production. The empty bus seat or unoccupied hotel room all represent opportunities which have been lost for ever. Unlike manufacturers of goods, service companies cannot keep on producing the service and store it up for future sales. For service industries, striking the right balance between capacity and sales can be extremely difficult, especially if demand is liable to fluctuate.

The problem of perishability has a number of implications if you sell services.

1 **Repeat business.** You should endeavour to maximize predictable demand by doing everything possible to cultivate a loyal customer base on whose regular purchases you can usually depend. A customer is a valuable asset to any company. To a service company he has even more value because he knows you, understands you and trusts you to provide a good service.

2 **Special promotions.** You will often have to use techniques such as price discrimination and sales promotion (see Chapters 9 and 10) to boost demand at slack times.

3 **Long-term and short-term promotional objectives.** As a service company you often need two very different sets of promotional objectives. On the one hand you need to use long-term, 'soft sell' methods of

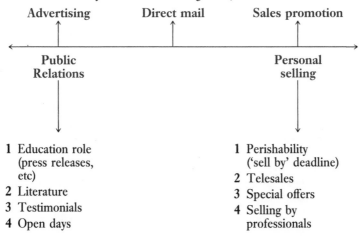

Fig. 7.6 Points of promotional emphasis for service marketers

promotion to build up the image of your service and reinforce the loyalty of existing customers. Therefore, you should devote resources to public relations techniques such as open days, brochures containing testimonials from well known, satisfied customers and examples of work you have done. Press releases should be used as extensively as possible. On the other hand, due to the problem of perishability, you need to attack the threat of spare capacity by the use of short-term, 'hard sell' techniques, sometimes promoting at the eleventh hour. This involves determined selling which must be persistent but must not harm your professional or 'user friendly' reputation.

Summary

1 For most companies it is unwise to have all your eggs in one basket because products do not have an indefinite life. You therefore need a range of products, at different stages in their life cycle, with a proportion of the profits from 'today's breadwinners' being invested in 'tomorrow's breadwinners'.

2 The new product development process is rife with potential pitfalls. Small companies must pay special attention to the danger of being subjective and should be prepared to seek objective information from the marketplace before incurring the high costs of developing, protecting and launching new products.

3 All products should be viewed in terms of the full package of benefits which they offer to customers rather than in terms of the core product or service only. It is often the value added services or even its brand image, which gives companies a competitive edge in the marketplace.

4 Goods and services are not intrinsically different. They are both products which must meet the needs or solve the problems of customers if they are to be successful. However, the intangibility, inseparability and perishability of services suggest that marginal adjustments to their marketing mix can pay dividends.

Action

Think of just one new way of adding value to your main product or service. Could you offer:

a a more extensive guarantee?
b an installation service? (it doesn't have to be free)
c a free manual of some kind?
d a free 'customer club'?
e an 'update service' covering new products, new developments or new events?

If you can think of just one additional benefit, and tell all past customers and good prospects about it, it will almost certainly bring you some new business.

8 Place

Aims of this chapter

'Place', or distribution, is all about the getting the right products to the right place, at the right time. Since many companies do not deal directly with the end users of their products, this element of the marketing mix can encompass a complex range of activities, individuals and organizations. This chapter will:

- Explain why distribution is such an important element in the marketplace
- Examine different methods of getting products to end users

The importance of distribution

Distribution is important to all businesses. There are three levels at which you must get your distribution right. They are shown in the following questions:

1 Is my product always available for customers to buy?
   Can customers buy it?

2 If it is available, is it more or less accessible than competing products?
   How easy is it for customers to buy it?

3 If it is available and accessible, how good is our customer service?
   How pleasant is it for customers to buy it?

Availability

If your product is not available, questions two and three above become irrelevant. Availability is therefore your first priority. This does not necessarily mean that you have to have weeks of stock available 'off the shelf'. In different industries there are different expectations of delivery times. Frequently purchased products have to be available whenever customers wish to buy, on the other hand some products are custom made, so customers expect to wait (within reason). If in doubt, you should assume that if your product is not constantly available, you will lose business.

Accessibility

Once you are satisfied that your company outperforms the competition on availability, you should turn your attention to the question of accessibility. Your product may be available, but how easy is it to buy in relation to your competitors' products? To tackle this question you need a thorough understanding of customers' purchasing behaviour and buying criteria: do they want to stroll round the corner to the nearest shop to buy the product, do they want to pick up the telephone and order instant delivery, or do they want demonstrations or trials? For many products, ease of purchase will override brand loyalty.

As a small firm, you have to question whether you can satisfy buyers' accessibility requirements from your own resources. If not, you will have to use middlemen to make your product more accessible (see page 115). Overestimating the prestige of your product or company can cause you to make errors regarding the accessibility of your business. Do not assume, without irrefutable evidence, that buyers will make long journeys, go out of their way, walk long distances from the nearest car park or venture into unfamiliar or unpleasant locations just to visit your premises. Many will not. Most buyers opt for easy, familiar and safe methods of purchase. They do not like difficulty, uncertainty or risk.

Service

If customers are satisfied on the questions of availability and accessibility it may well be the level of customer service offered by competing suppliers which most influences their purchase decision. There are two key factors which determine your company's ability to provide consistently good customer service.

1 Procedures. Many firms fail in their task of getting the right product to the right place at the right time because their procedures are not sufficiently clear or well organized to enable them to minimize administrative delays or foresee problems. In most businesses there are many activities which need to be coordinated between the stages of the customer placing his order and of finally receiving satisfaction. Somebody has to manage these activities, and has to do so through an efficient system which is clear enough for someone else to follow in the event of illness or holidays. Grants are available under the Financial and Information Systems section of the DTI's Enterprise Initiative scheme to help small firms with the cost of using an outside consultant to develop such a system. Details of the Enterprise Initiative are available from the DTI.

2 People. Systems are no better than the people who have to make them work, and if several people are involved they are no better than the weakest link. If the company has a good system but customer service problems still occur, they will almost certainly be due not to people's inability but to their lack of motivation. Through good management you can ensure that your staff are highly motivated to provide excellent customer service. There are three ways of improving the motivation of your staff in this respect.

a Training. Periodic training sessions ensure that all staff are fully aware of ordering procedures, are saying the right things and adopting the right manner on the telephone. They also enable all employees to make suggestions, raise any problems, avoid communication barriers and, as a result, help to motivate all staff to work together towards common goals.

b Involvement. People are always more committed to any cause if they have been fully consulted and involved in its development. If staff are involved in the development of customer service systems and procedures they will be much more likely to want to make those systems work. Regular customer service review meetings, involving all relevant staff, will improve teamwork and motivation.

c Example. Also important is the example set by owners, directors and other senior people. Junior staff will take their lead from senior staff. They will notice whether the boss appears to seek out or avoid contact with customers. They will notice whether he is prepared to drop everything in order to solve a problem for a customer. They will be influenced by even jocular comments about the customers. If a company is to develop a genuinely customer oriented culture, it must start at the top.

Alternative forms of distribution

This section analyses the alternative distribution channels through which you can provide availability, accessibility and service to your customers. These options are summarized in fig. 8.1 on the next page.

Direct marketing

Referring to channels 1 and 2 in the diagram, direct marketing involves the producer selling directly to the consumer. One method of reaching the consumer directly is mail order which can be promoted by direct response advertisements, catalogues and mailshots. Alternatively, you could use sales people to visit potential buyers and take orders. Telephone selling can also be used for this purpose, but usually only with existing customers. Meeting potential buyers in groups is a very efficient method of direct selling. This can be achieved through party plan events, booking stands at exhibitions, craft fairs or other suitable events, or by sponsoring your own event. Some firms develop their own showroom or factory shop so that customers can visit their premises to examine products, place orders and collect goods.

The advantages of direct marketing are:

1 Direct marketing has one great advantage over other channels of distribution, which no doubt explains its popularity amongst many small firms: it cuts out the middleman's percentage.

2 Some small firms are reluctant to deal with organizations which are much more powerful than themselves, and many retailers, wholesalers and industrial distributors do come into this category.

3 There are customers who prefer to buy direct from the manufacturer, either because they perceive a price advantage or because they like to deal with the 'expert'. This latter factor is most prevalent in hobby and special interest markets.

Although these three factors can offer sound reasons for opting for direct marketing, they must be compared with the disadvantages before a strategy is chosen.

The disadvantages of direct marketing are:

1 The chief disadvantage of direct marketing is the huge commitment of time and resources which is often required to do it properly. The lead generating and selling activities that have been outlined above are

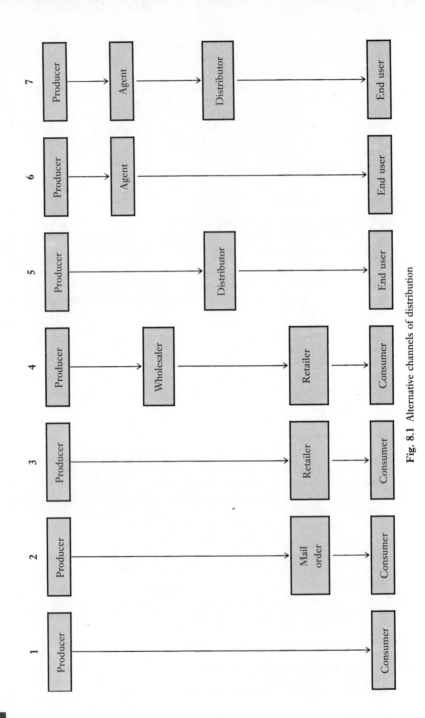

Fig. 8.1 Alternative channels of distribution

extremely time-consuming and expensive. It may well be that the margin you give to the distributor costs your company less than the marketing activities you would need to undertake to deal directly with the end user.

2 You must ask yourself whether you can reach as many potential customers directly as you could with the aid of middlemen. If there are parts of the country or parts of the market where your product could not be sold (or not sold well), you really need to consider using distributors.

3 In addition to availability, you must consider accessibility. How easy will it be for your customers to buy from you if you sell direct?

4 Many customers do not like the mail order method of purchasing because of its greater uncertainty. This uncertainty is magnified if the supplier is a small firm with little or no reputation in the marketplace.

Selling direct can be a feasible option for small firms operating in a relatively confined geographical area, or in some very specialized markets where retail outlets are uncommon. However, even under these circumstances you would be well advised to devote effort to taking your business to customers via exhibitions and other events rather than relying solely on customers taking the trouble or the risk of coming to you, either at your showroom or via mail order.

Using middlemen

Channels 3 to 7 in fig. 8.1 all involve the use of middlemen. The traditional channel of distribution in the retail world used to involve a relatively small number of wholesalers who served a vast number of small retailers. In recent years the corner shop has gradually yielded ground to the national chains who purchase straight from the producer, shown in channel 3. A more recent arrival on the retail scene is the out of town 'shed'. Shown in channel 5, this type of middleman is becoming increasingly difficult to distinguish from the traditional industrial distributor. In fact, many do-it-yourself, building and motor component distributors include both individuals and businesses amongst their customers. The agent, who appears in channels 6 and 7, is more usually found in the industrial sector. Unlike a distributor, an agent does not take title to the products he handles. If you are a small unknown company, an agent may represent your easiest route into a new market because he incurs less risk than a distributor, who would have to buy and stock your product. Since he takes less risk, the agent also costs less (usually 10 to 15 per cent commission on sales), which is more suitable for any firms who are themselves on tight margins. Some distributors, particularly in the retail world, will expect a 100 per cent mark-up.

The advantages and disadvantages of using middlemen are basically the converse of those for using direct marketing methods. On balance, most small firms who wish to grow will have to use middlemen because of the opportunity they afford to reach far wider markets. If you do plan to use middlemen, your relationship with them may not always be easy. Both the producer and the middleman are trying to maximize their profit out of the same product, which is potentially a direct source of conflict. Whereas you are only interested in sales of your own product, the middleman may stock hundreds or even thousands of lines, from which yours represents only a small priority. Essentially, middlemen are interested in only two things: making sales and making a good margin on those sales. Thus, if you, as a small producer, want to get the best out of your relationship with middlemen you need to recognize those two facts.

The following suggestions should help a small firm in its relationships with middlemen.

1 Work out your costings very carefully and give your middlemen the best margin you can reasonably afford. If your product offers better margins than competing products which they stock, most middlemen would push your product.

2 Invest in some promotional activities which are directed to end users with the objective of encouraging end users to demand your product from the middlemen.

3 Make sure your middlemen have all the necessary product or technical knowledge which they require to sell your product effectively.

4 Make sure you know who your end users are. You can do this by including a warranty which the purchaser has to fill in and return to the manufacturer. This user list may identify a useful market for selling spares or servicing, for example. As future potential buyers they form a useful audience for promotion and research activities. If you sell lower value consumables you can run on-pack competitions with mini questionnaires which could help you to build up a picture of the kind of people who buy your product.

5 Many middlemen do not like their suppliers to sell direct. If middlemen are to form an important part of your marketing strategy it would be wise to consult with them before engaging in direct marketing activities. However, provided you would not offend any important distributors you could consider using a combination of channels to reach your market.

6 Last but not least, if you do use middlemen remember that they are your customers and you should see them and treat them as such. You should keep close contact through visits and by telephone and you should ensure that they are happy with the products and the service they are receiving.

Summary

1 Unless you are certain that you have a unique, high prestige product, you should aim for off-the-shelf availability or delivery times better than the industry average.

2 Accessibility is crucial in many purchase decisions. People are not prepared to incur inconvenience or uncertainty in the purchase of most products.

3 Without good customer service, no business will win the long-term loyalty of customers. Good customer service depends on clear and efficient systems and on highly motivated staff.

4 Direct marketing often appears to be an attractive option for small firms but it involves extensive costs, a lot of time, and it may reduce the availability and accessibility of your product in the eyes of customers.

5 Provided you can build the distributor's margins into your own costings, use of middlemen will enable your business to grow by reaching new markets.

6 If you use distributors you should see them as customers and you should attempt to organize your business to meet their needs.

Action

1 How easy is it for customers to buy your product compared with competing products? Write down all your advantages and disadvantages as far as accessibility is concerned. Could you promote your advantages more? How can you overcome your disadvantages?

2 If you are considering direct marketing as a method of distribution:

a list the methods you will use to reach potential customers

b estimate the annual cost of these activities

c as a proportion of your expected sales (or historic sales if you already pursue this strategy), how does this figure compare with the margin you would need to give distributors?

3 If you use middlemen:

a when did you last visit them to ask how well your company meets their needs?

b do you have any method of identifying the end users who buy your products?

c do you undertake any promotional activities which are aimed at end users?

9 Pricing

Aims of this chapter

> 'Costing is a matter of fact. Pricing is a matter of policy.'

Pricing: an activity which should be led by marketing; rather than costing, an activity which should be carried out by accountants. Of course, to fix a price you need full knowledge of your costings but pricing, like all other marketing activities, must be driven by an outward looking perception rather than by inward looking priorities. This chapter will examine:

- The long-term factors which should be considered when determining pricing strategy
- The role of pricing as a short-term tactical tool
- Practical considerations in the management of your pricing

Pricing strategy

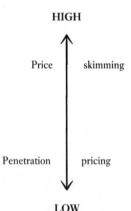

Fig. 9.1 Where do you lie on the pricing scale?

In theory, firms have an unlimited choice of pricing possibilities. They can choose to charge a very high price, probably reducing their volume of sales, but increasing the amount of profit made on each sale. This 'price skimming' strategy skims the cream from the market by identifying those customers who are prepared to pay a premium price for a product which, they feel, precisely meets their needs. At the other end of the pricing scale, firms can choose to charge a very low price. Known as a 'penetration pricing' strategy, its objective is usually to penetrate the market, and gain market share. The resultant high volume sales, together with the beneficial effects of economies of scale on the firm's unit costs, are often held to outweigh the very low profit margins which will inevitably arise from such a pricing strategy. This section will examine the factors you should take into account when you are determining your position on the pricing scale.

Costs

To arrive at the best possible pricing decision for your company you need to have a detailed understanding of your own cost structure. As a minimum requirement, most firms will want to establish a base line for each product or service offered, below which the firm cannot trade without making a loss. Small business owners should ensure that they understand the following fundamentals of their own internal cost structure.

1 **Profit contribution by product.** How much money does each of your product or service lines make for your company? Such information is essential if you are going to be able to analyse your products in terms of 'yesterday's, today's and tomorrow's breadwinners'. Penetration pricing strategies, for example, may have a useful role to play in the development of 'tomorrow's breadwinners'. For 'yesterday's breadwinners,' however, a price skimming strategy should be considered, because unless they can make a good profit contribution in the short term, they are of little value to the company.

2 **Profit margins by product.** It is also essential to know the profit margin of each product line. What would be the effect of changes in price, sales volume or costs on the profit contribution made by each product? For example, for some low margin product lines, a very tiny price rise can have a strongly positive effect on that product's profit contribution. This will be discussed further, later in the chapter.

3 Costs and value. A detailed breakdown of the main cost element for each product line will help managers to identify areas where economies can be made if intense competition in the marketplace begins to exert downward pressure on prices. In the long run, it is difficult to be competitive if you have higher costs than your main rivals. You must, therefore, take a healthy interest in the cost structure of each of your products or service lines.

However, you must be more concerned with the relationship between cost to the company and value to the customer. Along with a list of the main areas of cost to the company in offering a particular product line to the marketplace, you should be clear about the main aspects of value which that product offers to customers. Cost reduction which results from improved internal efficiency and does not affect the value package offered to customers can only improve the firm's competitiveness. However, beware of cost-cutting where your costs are lowered through a reduction in the level of service or other benefits offered to customers. Few things do more damage to a company's reputation than to be seen to be skimping at the customer's expense.

Objectives

If costing is a matter of fact, but pricing is a matter of policy, then the firm's cost structure alone will not determine the pricing decision. Other factors will be very important. The first of these factors is the firm's objectives and there are three main ways in which company objectives can influence the pricing decision.

a High value. Some firms wish to position themselves at the high value, high quality end of the market. If so, higher than average prices will be necessary for two reasons. Firstly, if you are going to offer higher value than your competitors you will almost certainly incur some additional costs. If you want to make a good profit, these higher costs will have to be reflected in your prices. Secondly, price, like other aspects of your marketing mix, communicates messages to customers about the kind of company you are and the kind of product or service you sell. If you offer high value and high quality, most customers expect your prices to be higher than average.

b Buying market share. Some firms adopt a penetration strategy, which involves setting very competitive prices in the hope of gaining market share. If successful, it is believed that the ensuing higher volumes of sales will compensate for the lower profit margins achieved on each sale. This can be a very dangerous policy for small firms to pursue. Very often, they do not achieve the kind of economies of scale which make a real impact on their costs. Also, the volume of additional sales that you must achieve to compensate for even small reductions in price and profit margins can be extremely high.

The table opposite shows the amount of sales increase you need to make to cover a given price reduction, if you wish to maintain your profits at their pre-price reduction level. The result is dependent on your profit margins. If you already operate on low profit margins, a very large increase in sales will be required to compensate for even a small price cut. For example, if your profit margin is 20 per cent (your variable cost as a percentage of sales is 80 per cent) you will see by following the second column from the right hand side, that you would need to increase your sales by one third to cover a 5 per cent price reduction. Unless they operate on very high margins, most firms will find it very difficult to increase their sales by a sufficient amount to compensate for all but the smallest of price reductions.

Conversely, the table shows the scope which exists for increasing profits through relatively small price increases. If you operate on very low margins, a tiny price rise can bring significant benefits. The right hand column of the table shows that if you operate on 10 per cent profit margins you would have to suffer a relatively large fall in sales to wipe out the benefits of any price rise.

c Spare capacity. Sometimes, when they have spare capacity due to a shortage of work, firms feel that, at least in the short term, they should seek work at virtually any price in order to keep the factory busy and avoid laying off employees. They may therefore adopt a 'marginal costing' policy which seeks to cover the variable costs of a job but not the full cost. A contribution is thus made to overheads. For the marketing of services, this policy is often a deliberate and integral part of a company's strategy, for example, cheaper meals in restaurants on Monday nights. However, from a marketing of products point of view you should approach a marginal costing policy with extreme caution because customers will remember low

Variable cost as a % of sales	10	20	30	40	50	60	70	80	90
Price reductions as a % of sales	Sales volume increase (%) required to maintain profit contribution								
1	1.1	1.3	1.5	2.0	2.1	2.6	3.5	5.3	11.1
2½	2.9	3.2	3.7	4.3	5.3	6.7	9.1	14.3	33.3
5	5.9	6.7	7.7	9.1	11.1	14.3	20.0	33.3	100.0
7½	9.1	10.3	12.0	14.3	17.7	23.1	33.3	60.0	300.0
10	12.5	14.3	16.7	20.0	25.0	33.3	50.0	100.0	
12½	16.1	18.5	21.7	26.3	33.3	45.4	71.4	166.7	
15	20.0	23.1	27.2	33.3	42.8	60.0	100.0	300.0	
17½	24.1	28.0	33.3	41.2	53.8	77.8	140.0	700.0	
20	28.6	33.3	40.0	50.0	66.7	100.0	200.0		
25	38.5	45.4	55.5	71.4	100.0	166.7	500.0		
30	50.0	60.0	75.0	100.0	150.0	300.0			
33	58.7	71.2	90.8	125.0	200.0	500.0			
35	63.6	77.7	100.0	140.0	233.3	700.0			
40	80.0	100.0	133.3	200.0	400.0				
45	100.0	128.5	180.0	300.0	900.0				
50	125.0	166.7	250.0	500.0					
Variable cost as a % of sales	10	20	30	40	50	60	70	80	90

Loss line

Fig. 9.2 The relationship between price reductions, sales increases and variable costs

prices and you may be making it very difficult for yourself to charge even reasonable prices at a later date.

Demand

Whatever your costs and whatever the firm's objectives, demand in the marketplace must exert a significant influence on your pricing decision. When demand for a product exceeds supply, sellers find it easier to charge higher prices. In industries suffering from overcapacity with supply exceeding demand, buyers are in a much stronger position, and through shopping around they will often be able to exert strong downward pressure on industry prices. If you are locked into an industry with extreme overcapacity your freedom to develop your own pricing strategy may be severely curtailed.

If you are in a market showing strong demand it may still be wise to exercise restraint when determining your pricing strategy. Charge high prices for a high value product or service, but resist the temptation to take advantage of customers by charging prices which appear excessive. If new suppliers emerge you will lose any customers who feel that they have been unfairly treated in any way.

An additional factor to take into account is the 'elasticity of demand'. Demand for some products will be more elastic (sensitive) in the face of price changes than it will for other products. There are some products that customers have to buy. Total demand for such products will be relatively inelastic (unchanging) in response to price changes. If you face strong competition, you may find unilateral price rises difficult to sustain. Many firms, however, face relatively little direct competition in their niche of the market and attempt to appeal to customers through other factors, for example, a more convenient location or superior after sales service terms. For buyers of some products the cost of shopping around and changing suppliers may be greater than the cost of just accepting small price increases.

Therefore, the level and the extent of demand in the marketplace can have a great impact on your freedom or lack of freedom to set your prices. It is difficult to estimate demand in many cases. If you know your market well, a 'gut feeling' can be a useful guide. The stage of the product in its life cycle (see Chapter 7) is a useful indicator. If you think market demand would allow you to charge higher prices, you might test or research your ideas before implementing a full-scale price rise.

Competitors

Many firms allow themselves to be strongly influenced by competitors' prices when determining their own price levels. Of course, you must keep a keen eye on your rivals' prices, particularly if you sell a product or service for which customers are known to compare prices before reaching a purchase decision. (*NB* Only objective market research will uncover the extent to which customers really shop around. Firms often overestimate the price sensitivity of their customers.)

Competition-oriented pricing can be very dangerous, leading sometimes to rash price-cutting and a downward spiral in prices which can affect the whole of the industry. Firms instead should devote more management effort to differentiating themselves from the competition thus giving themselves more latitude on pricing decisions, and less effort on matching or beating competitors' prices. Research evidence suggests that many firms put price pressure on themselves, selling at prices lower than they need to. Most customers are more interested in a good value package which meets their needs than in a slightly lower price.

Distributors

1 **Powerful distributors.** If you sell through distributors they may have a very powerful effect on your pricing strategy. Small firms supplying large distributors often have little freedom in designing their own pricing strategies. The distributor will fix the retail price, will know his own mark-up requirements and may thus virtually dictate price terms to his small suppliers. In this situation you have only three management options. Firstly, you should always try very hard to negotiate the suggested price upwards. If your margins are low, even tiny price increases can be extremely valuable. Secondly, you should ensure that your own internal costings are very detailed and very accurate. You may find that your lucrative looking contract with the large retailer involves a tremendous amount of work for very little profit. If so, what could your firm achieve if it liberated those management and production resources for other purposes? Thirdly, short payment terms, prompt invoicing and efficient collection can be extremely important.

2 **Smaller distributors.** If you trade with smaller distributors you may have much more freedom with your pricing strategy. The important thing to remember is the smaller distributors also have to make a living. They may not be powerful enough to negotiate down your prices, but if your competitors' products offer them a better margin they will obviously prefer to promote those products. These distributors are your customers. You need to understand their needs and to maintain close relationships with them.

3 **A price band.** All of the factors outlined so far in this section will influence your pricing strategy. Consideration of all these should enable you to arrive at an appropriate price band for each of your product or service lines. This band may have your ideal, profit maximizing, price as an upper limit, and, as a lower limit, a price below which it is not viable for you to trade. Your pricing strategy has thus fixed the parameters within which you are prepared to use price as a short-term tactical tool in your day-to-day marketing management.

Pricing tactics

Within your price band you may choose to alter prices as conditions change or with the aim of securing a short-term advantage over the competition. Three commonly used tactical pricing techniques are now outlined.

Promotional discounts

Short-term promotional discounts, often known as sales promotions in consumer markets, are a very commonly used method of cutting prices in the hope of stimulating extra sales. Such sales promotions could, for example, include a 10 per cent price cut across the board for a limited period, price reductions on selected items, an end of season sale or a free product offered to an important customer. Before entering into such promotions, however, it is advisable to clarify your motives.

1 **Cash flow.** There is evidence that short-term promotional discounts do have a beneficial effect on cash flow, particularly in consumer markets. A sale or a special offer will often serve as a short-term incentive to buy. Discounts can also be used to encourage trade customers to settle bills quickly, for example, offering a 2.5 per cent discount for payment within seven days. However, do remember that short-term cash flow gains may be counterbalanced by reduced takings in a later period.

2 **Sales.** There is much evidence that although sales may increase short-term sales, they do not increase most firms' long-term sales. Many people stock up with special offer items because there is a saving over the normal price. However, as far as most products are concerned they do not actually consume more. Thus, in the period following the promotion, sales will often fall as consumers use up their stocks, leaving the firm with little, if any net gain in sales.

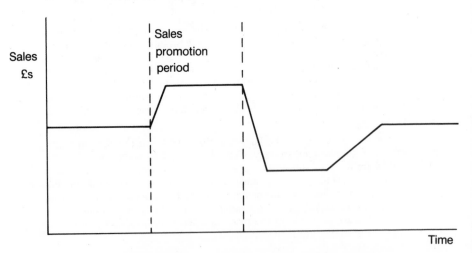

Fig. 9.3 The effect of promotional discounts on sales and cash flow

Some products, however, do show longer term sales gains. If you believe you have a product which people would like and buy regularly if only you could tempt them to an initial purchase, a well designed sales promotion may yield a long-term increase in sales. However, do not overestimate the number of converts you will make.

3 Profits. It is very unwise for most firms to look upon promotional discounts as a way of increasing their profits. Unless you can hide the discounts from your existing customers, which is not usually possible, sales promotions actually give money away by subsidizing the purchases of regular customers. By checking with fig. 9.2 you can work out the amount by which you need to increase your sales to improve your profits as a result of a promotional discount.

4 Competition. Many firms offer promotional discounts as a way of winning business from their competitors but frequently these tactics prove unsuccessful. In markets for regularly purchased products, whether industrial or consumer, a price discount may induce short-term switching by buyers. However, the promotional discount will also subsidize existing customers, thus leading to a reduction in profits, even if sales do temporarily rise. If the short-term switchers return to their normal supplier after the promotion ends (which they often do), nothing will have been gained from the sales promotion. It may even be harmful if regular customers then resent the 'price increase' at the end of the promotional period.

Generally speaking, the way to beat the competition is through offering added value, not cutting costs. In the long run you will only win and keep new customers if you meet their needs more closely than they are met by your competitors.

Price discrimination

Price discrimination means charging different prices to different customers. This pricing tactic is particularly suited to service companies who cannot store up their 'product' but must try to sell their whole 'supply' each day. If a hotel, for example, does not let all their rooms on any particular day, it has lost that potential revenue forever. Many companies therefore introduce special pricing schemes, often marginally costed, to try to attract business which they would not have gained through normal trading. Standby tickets on airlines are a good example of price discrimination. If you feel that some kind of discrimination pricing could be of benefit to your business there are three crucial points to bear in mind:

1 Precise costings. If you see price discrimination as a way of winning marginal business, you need to be absolutely certain that you are actually making money out of the operation. You need to be certain that all your variable (or operating) costs are well covered and that the additional business is making a worthwhile contribution to overheads. There is no point doing it just to keep everybody busy. You also need to be sure that all your overheads are fully covered by normal business if you plan to pursue marginal costing policies.

2 Targeting. Any discriminatory pricing needs to be very carefully targeted at specific segments. If a company chooses to reduce prices, but only for a specific target market, there is the danger that those regular customers in a non-targeted area will object to paying the unreduced price. You have to make sure that each segment knows what it is getting and that the customers paying the higher price realize that they are in some way benefiting by not paying the unreduced price. For example, a hotel may cut its bed and breakfast price by a significant margin for 'same day' bookings from casual visitors. This would attract additional business and fill any spare capacity but would not offend regular price customers who prefer the security of advance booking.

3 Added value. An alternative way of viewing price discrimination is to offer a higher value-added package rather than a price cut as a way of attracting additional business. If the added benefits are carefully matched with the needs of specific segments, the total package can often be more attractive to potential customers than a lower price – and it should be better for your profits. For example, hotels arrange 'bargain break' packages with special themes, the theme aimed at a particular segment of the market.

Psychological pricing

If the pricing analysis of a new product shows that it should retail at £10, it will most likely actually retail at £9.99. Research studies have shown that it does make a difference to overall sales. Very often people are tempted to buy something but need to convince themselves that it is a good idea. In such circumstances they will concentrate on the £9 part of the price rather than the additional 99p!

Managing price

However well thought out your pricing strategy and tactics, it is still essential to keep a firm grip on the day-to-day implementation of pricing decisions.

Managing price changes

In an age of continuous inflation price changes usually mean price rises, which are often necessary on an annual basis. The first point to make is that if a firm cannot absorb increases in costs, those increases must be passed on to customers, assuming that the firm does not wish to make reduced profits. In this situation, the challenge facing the businessman is to minimize the disadvantages of the price rise in the marketplace. Firstly, it is essential to communicate the price rise to customers. Much goodwill can be lost if customers find out about the increase through, say, a larger invoice. Secondly, the increase can be justified, perhaps through inflation, perhaps through the effect of a weak pound on the price of imported raw materials or through any reason which customers will appreciate. Thirdly, if you are worried about the market acceptability of the higher price, it could be accompanied by an additional benefit such as improved deliveries, or a new after sales service package. It must always be remembered that it is rarely the price alone on which customers base their purchase decision but the total value package on offer from the supplier.

Customers' reactions to price changes will also be affected by many other factors. People are more price sensitive with some purchases than others. For example, they are generally sensitive to price increases when products are already perceived as expensive or are bought frequently whereas they may hardly notice price rises on small or already lower priced items which they do not buy very often.

Consistent pricing

Once you have agreed on a price rise or a particular pricing policy, you should pursue it consistently. Many firms are tempted to use price cuts or discounts as a way of gaining business. Such tactics often backfire. Customers tend to draw the conclusion that the price-cutter is desperate for business and price haggling is encouraged. Equally, when negotiating with individual customers, a price discount should never be offered, except as a last resort, when all other avenues to a sale have been closed, and, even then, the offer of a discount should be traded for something of value, such as prompt payment or a larger order. It is always preferable to sell a high value package for a good price. Customers rarely value cheapness and price-cutting.

Prompt settlement

Your company's financial health can depend not only on your ability to charge an adequate price for the goods or services you supply, but also on your efficiency in administering sales. Prompt invoicing, short payment terms and firm (but polite) debt collection can have a huge impact on the company's cash flow. All staff must be highly efficient in processing sales orders and firm in upholding payment terms. It is very easy for sales staff to offer extended credit or to overlook late payment. Some customers will take advantage of such leniency. Most customers will respect rather than resent the supplier who clearly spells out his terms of business and then politely but firmly adheres to them. It is not unheard of for powerful customers to take advantage of small firms, so it pays to be very strict with your terms and conditions.

Summary

1 Firms should develop a pricing strategy which takes into account internal costs, the company's marketing objectives, the strength and nature of demand in the marketplace, competitors' prices and distributors' requirements.

2 Within the band established by the pricing strategy, price may be used as a short-term tactical tool to boost cash flow, to fill spare capacity or to promote certain product lines.

3 It is important to appreciate the trade-off between costs and value. Instead of seeking to minimize their costs and charge the most competitive prices, firms should explore higher price, higher value added packages. Research has shown that higher value products tend to be more successful than their bargain basement competitors.

Action

Draw up and complete a table similar to the one below for your company's products for the past financial year.

	Sales	Total profit contribution	Gross profit margin
Product A			
Product B			
Product C			
(*and so on*)			

a does your firm have any products in its range whose absolute profit contribution is so small that they are of little value to the company?

b does your firm have any products with high sales and low net margins which consume a disproportionate amount of the firm's resources compared to the profit they make?

c is there any possibility of adding value to your low margin products which would enable you to increase your prices and returns?

d which of your products show the highest gross margins? Are you doing everything you can to maximize sales of these products?

10 Promotion

Aims of this chapter

In today's highly competitive markets the need for marketing communications is constantly growing. Selling has become a science: exhibitions are big business, brochures are getting glossier, buyers are bombarded with advertising messages in magazines, through the post and on television and radio, PR and telephone selling are widely used and new promotional opportunities such as videos and satellite television continue to emerge.

This chapter will consider how you can get your message across to potential customers by examining:

- How to communicate effectively
- How to get the best out of specific promotional techniques

How to communicate effectively

Marketing is about three things:

1 Finding out what customers want.

2 Organizing your business to provide what they want.

Fig. 10.1 Dual meaning?

3 Telling them that you do it. Making the customer aware of what your company offers can be the most challenging part of the whole process, because in today's very crowded marketplace it can be extremely difficult to engage their attention. Therefore, before examining specific promotional techniques it is important to consider why it is so difficult to get your message across, and how you can best overcome the problem.

Poor communication

Communicating is not easy. Even talking to someone face to face can be difficult. Misunderstandings occur frequently, often because words and phrases have more than one meaning, which causes people to interpret them in different ways.

Problems with marketing communications

The chief cause of most problems with marketing communications is the fact that they generally do not involve face to face contact. They involve sending messages through various kinds of media (such as newspapers, television or letters) to a remote audience. Fig. 10.2 illustrates this 'one-way' communications process.

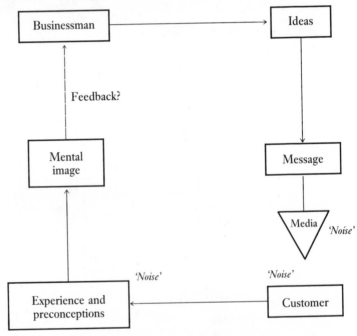

Fig. 10.2 One-way marketing communications

The problems with this process are shown in the following example. The businessman, who sells fax machines, wishes to communicate with a target audience (small companies, not very knowledgeable about fax machines) and has a head full of ideas about the benefits of these machines. But if the businessman wants to communicate with potential customers via an advert, he must organize his head full of ideas into some kind of message which will fit into the space he has available for his advert. This involves 'changing' the message, from a collection of thoughts into printed text. The advertisement is then sent to its audience through one or several media. But, the type of medium used may influence the way the message is interpreted by the public. For instance, an advert in the *The Sun* may not be taken in the same way as an identical advert in *The Guardian*. The small business person reading the fax machine ad in *Management Today* might be inclined to jump to the conclusion that 'fax machines are just for large companies' whereas if he saw the same advert in his small business association magazine he might be more inclined to think, 'well, perhaps fax machines are for small businesses'.

Another problem with the marketing process is that the audience may misunderstand the message that is being advertised. For example, the famous drink advertisement featuring Joan Collins and Leonard Rossiter was for Cinzano, but many thought it was advertising Martini.

Whatever the medium the biggest danger is that many people in the target audience will not even notice the advert in the first place, such are the volume and 'loudness' of competitors for their attention. Other adverts and editorial copy in the magazine, other magazines, distractions and interruptions or just pressure of business all take the attention of the audience away from the advert. And the portion of the audience which does give the advert its undivided attention does not necessarily take in the total message. Anyone unfamiliar with facsimile technology will struggle to understand the advert. They will have to translate it into concepts which fit in with their own experience or preconceptions of fax machines. As a result of this translating process the message undergoes yet another change. After its long journey, the mental image formed by the customer is often dependent on the individual's expectations and preconceptions. As a result, several individuals can interpret the same message in different ways. The danger is that the message which has been formed in the minds of some customers will bear little resemblance to the businessman's original collection of thoughts. Depending on the extent to which he has incorporated 'feedback' into the process (for example, by encouraging responses or questioning customers about the advert) he may or may not be aware of his success rate.

The communications dilemma

This model of the marketing communications process highlights the two key threats to the promotion of all businesses. Quite simply they are:

1 Getting your message noticed at all.
2 Getting the right message noticed.

This is the dilemma of '**impact** versus **understanding**'. The most obvious threat in the process is 'noise'. It has been estimated that the average person is exposed to over 1000 selling messages every day, in the form of adverts, mailshots, roadside posters, etc. Most people react to this information overload by subconsciously closing their minds to the vast majority of these messages. As a result, firms are tempted to resort to 'gimmicks' to get their message noticed. However, many gimmicky advertisements fail because customers do not remember the intended message – they remember the gimmick instead.

Alfred Politz, a well known American adman, wrote this now famous fable in 1960.

> 'Imagine a room with a large window that looks out on beautiful countryside. On the wall opposite the window are three mirrors. The first mirror is uneven, spotted and dirty looking. The second mirror is clean, neat and, in addition, is framed by a beautiful ornamental engraving. The third mirror has no frames or ornament, and is nothing but a plain, but perfectly flawless mirror. Now, an observer is taken into the room, and his guide points in turn to the three mirrors and asks "What do you see?" The observer replies firstly "I see a bad mirror", secondly "I see a beautiful mirror", and thirdly "I see a beautiful scene out of the open window".'

Politz's view is that it is the function of a good advert (or a good marketing communication), like a good mirror, to reflect with perfect clarity and perfect accuracy the subject (product) in question without attracting attention to itself. Politz also maintains that 'if a product has features worth paying money for it must also have features worth paying attention to'. The conclusion is inescapable: **keep your marketing communications clear and simple.**

Checklist: Communicating effectively

1 Communication is difficult enough face to face but is even more formidable when you are trying to communicate *en masse* with a remote audience.

2 This audience (your potential customers) is already being bombarded with thousands of other promotional messages and will therefore have little attention or memory space to devote to yours.

3 Gimmicks designed to attract attention should not be allowed to reduce clarity and simplicity.

 4 Therefore, to be understood, your promotional messages must be clear and simple.

How to advertise effectively

What is advertising?

Advertising is the sending of one promotional message through an advertising medium (such as a magazine) to reach a large target audience. It is impersonal. Assuming they see it, everyone in the target audience is exposed to the same message. Space or time is usually limited because of the high cost of most media, therefore advertising messages are usually brief and simple. Advertising, therefore, is the mass communication of simple messages.

Where can you advertise and at what cost?

There are many ways of sending advertising messages to your target audience. The advantages, disadvantages and the costs of the main media now follow.

1 **Newspapers**. There are national, regional and local newspapers, dailies and Sundays, paid for and free newspapers. Some are in colour, most are still in black and white but they all carry lots of advertisements.

The advantages of newspaper advertising are:

a Coverage. Newspapers are often an excellent way of covering a high percentage of the population. This is particularly true of local markets, especially in those areas which have free weekly newspapers which are delivered door to door to every house. If you want to reach a wide cross section of the community, newspapers would be a very cost-effective medium.

b Frequency. Newspapers are published frequently and have short lead times. You can therefore use them to send urgent advertising messages at short notice or to change your message frequently.

c Features. Most newspapers have regular features, such as womens' pages and special features, such as entertainment in the region over a bank holiday weekend. Such features, which are scheduled well in advance by newspapers, offer a useful way to reach specific market segments.

d Classified. Virtually all newspapers have classified advertising sections. The classified ads often have a very high readership, particularly in local and regional evening papers. If they have a clear index and a well marked section which you find your product or service will fall into, then they can be very cost-effective.

e Colour supplements. An increasing number of colour supplements are now an integral part of many newspapers. They offer high quality colour and are often read more leisurely than newspapers. They can be ideal for mail order fashion products, leisure products such as books, or smaller technical products.

f Split runs. Some newspapers and colour supplements offer split runs. The print run is often (but not always) split geographically which means that you can target the most appropriate region for your product. More importantly, for firms planning a run of adverts, it allows different adverts to be placed in the two split runs on the same day. This means you can test different copy, different photos, different sizes and different positions – but only test one major change at once. Having discovered a successful advertising format you can then repeat it until its effectiveness begins to decline.

g Repeats. Since newspapers are published regularly and have large circulations, you can often repeat the same advertisement over many weeks or even months, with little or no reduction in effectiveness.

The disadvantages of newspaper advertising are:

a Poor targeting. If you sell specialized products which are bought by only a small section of the community, especially if you sell nationally, newspaper advertising will often be wasteful. You would be paying to reach a very large number of people, only a small proportion of whom were likely to be potential customers.

b Poor impact. It is more difficult to make adverts stand out in newspapers than it is in many other media. Moreover, newspapers are usually skimmed through by readers, further reducing the chances of their noticing your ad. Free newspapers exacerbate this problem by having a higher proportion of advertisements than editorial content.

c Short life. Most newspapers have a very short life: dailies are typically thrown away the following day. However, local weeklies can pull in responses for two or three weeks after publication.

The White House Hotel
Cost-effective advertising to a distant audience

Pam and Ian Seabridge own the White House Hotel in Newquay, Cornwall. Its capacity of 55 guests is easily filled during the peak summer holiday months but the secret of profitability in that industry is to maximize early and late season bookings. With a good product (the hotel itself and the resort), Pam and Ian had to utilize other aspects of the marketing mix to achieve their objectives. With the overheads covered by the full-cost peak summer business, the White House could afford to adopt marginal costing tactics during the low season, resulting in a very attractive value for money package for the customers. As a further incentive the White House decided to run its own coaches from locations in the Midlands, providing visitors with virtually a door to door service. Pam and Ian then had to promote their package. They used the national press, with some small semi-display boxes in the holidays section of *The Mail on Sunday*, although they found that, at £67 per single column centimetre single column box, this was quite expensive. However, despite a circulation of almost two million, the results were disappointing. Careful monitoring of the responses showed that the value of bookings from this source was barely keeping pace with the cost of the advertising. At the other extreme, local weeklies such as *The Derbyshire Times* and *The Matlock Mercury* were tried. Once more, results were disappointing.

It was their use of the regional press that made the campaign successful. Targeting the Birmingham and Derby conurbations, small semi-display ads were placed in two regional newspapers: *The Sunday Mercury*, offering a single column centimetre price of £7.20 for a circulation of 55,000, and *The Derby Evening Telegraph*, offering a single column centimetre price of £5.30 for a circulation of 76,000. For a weekly advertising cost of around £50, short campaigns were run to target early and late holidaymakers. The other advantage of these regional dailies were the short lead times. Once a coach was filled from one of the locations, the campaign could be halted immediately.

The combination of the price, the coach and well targeted advertising resulted in a very cost-effective campaign, filling the White House with groups from Derbyshire and the West Midlands for several weeks during the low season.

This case study demonstrates the importance of careful experimentation to discover the most cost-effective way of advertising your product or service. Different media will be appropriate to different companies – the case study opposite showed the regional press to be very cost-effective.

The cost of newspaper advertising. The cost of newspaper advertising increases according to two very simple criteria. The bigger the space you book, the higher the cost, and the larger the circulation of the newspaper the more you will pay for any given space. Adverts can be divided into display and classified. Display ads are large advertisements which appear throughout the paper. The advertiser can design any message format he likes within the confines of the space booked. Display space is booked in terms of full pages or parts of pages (half, quarter, etc). The classified ads are usually small and placed together with other adverts. Space is sold in terms of single column centimetres (SCCs). For example, a 10 × 2 space would form an advert two columns wide and 10 cms deep. Within that space you can often use simple graphics. Basic classifieds offer only text and are usually priced by the line. Costs vary dramatically according to the two criteria of space and circulation, as shown by the examples below.

The Daily Mail
Full page £24,500
SCC £82
The Holme Valley Express
Full page £400
SCC £1.60

Costs will also vary according to other factors such as the ad's position in the newspaper. The front and back pages will be most expensive. Other prime spots, such as the television page, will also command a premium price. Lack of competition from other ads also increases the price, so a 'solus' spot (no other advertising on that page) or a 'next matter' position (next to editorial matter rather than surrounded by other adverts) will be more expensive than a 'run of paper' spot which the editor can place anywhere he wishes.

Cost-effectiveness. The higher cost of special positions or shapes will often be repaid in the form of greater effectiveness. It is generally accepted by advertising experts that the front page is the best, followed by the back. Then come the first two pages inside the front and the first two pages inside the back. After that, the nearer the front the better and right hand pages are generally more noticed than left hand ones. Also, the outside of any page is better than the 'gutter' (the fold down the middle). Regular features such as television, sport, letters or horoscope pages can do very well, particularly if you can match your target audience with typical readers of those pages.

Timing. Timing can also affect effectiveness. It is generally considered that for most products winter is a better time to advertise than summer. January and February are the best months (more newspapers are bought and read more thoroughly). Public holidays are particularly bad. December is risky because of the sheer volume of advertising, so avoid it unless Christmas sales are very important to you.

Different days of the week can also vary in their effectiveness. To discover which publications, times, sizes and ad styles work best, you have to experiment, and monitor the results carefully. But experiment cautiously. Start off by using media that are used by other people selling products like yours, then experiment gradually, changing only one factor at once. When you discover a successful formula stick with it until its effectiveness is clearly declining.

Expert Tuition: effective advertising to a local audience

Expert Tuition is a Chester-based home tuition agency run by ex-teachers Sheila and Bob Mitchell. The firm provides home tuition in a range of subjects from its large databank of qualified teachers. Now that the firm is successfully established it knows that it can rely on word of mouth to generate sufficient enquiries. Satisfied customers recommend the agency to friends, and families often return to the agency as younger brothers and sisters reach crucial stages in their school careers. Therefore, having no desire to expand further, Sheila and Bob spend very little on promotional activities. However, in their early days they had to advertise to make potential customers aware of their agency. Moreover, having little experience of advertising they had to experiment. They tried different ad styles and sizes and three different types of advertising media, and kept a record of the results they achieved. The media they used were: local weekly newspapers, regional daily newspapers (usually evening), and directories.

They found that the least costly of those media, the local weekly newspapers, were by far the most cost-effective. However, they also found that they could significantly improve their results from the local weeklies through a little careful planning. For example, they always chose newspapers which had a home tuition section in its advertising pages and they paid a little extra to ensure that their ad was always the first to appear in that section and that it was slightly more prominent than its competitors. Since most competitors booked only the cheapest form of classified ad, this involved paying for no more extras than a bold first line and one line gaps above and below the ad. As you can see from the example below, the wording of their most successful ad is clear, simple and to the point:

TUITION in all subjects
at all levels
Expert Tuition Agency. Tel: Chester 234567

The cost of this ad in the classified section of the Chester Chronicle series of local newspapers (there are about 10 different editions for local towns, for example, Crewe Chronicle, Northwich Chronicle) was around £20 per week. They were generating an average of 13 replies per week at an average cost of £1.50 per reply. As a buyer of home tuition would probably remain a loyal customer for years, and recommend Expert Tuition to other people, that was a very small promotional price to pay.

The lessons that can be learnt from Expert Tution's advertising experiences include:

1 The primary objective with advertising is to place it in a medium which is likely to be consulted by people who are considering buying a product like yours.

2 To find the right medium you often have to experiment at first.

3 It is only by monitoring replies and keeping accurate records that you will be able to compare the cost-effectiveness of different forms of promotion. If you know what each sales lead is costing you and you know what, on average, a new customer is worth to your company, it is easy to work out if your advertising is paying for itself, and, indeed, whether it would pay to spend more.

2 Magazines. There are thousands of magazines published in the United Kingdom, from very general magazines with a wide readership, such as the *Radio Times* to highly specialized journals with much smaller circulations. Some are published weekly, others quarterly or monthly.

The advantages of magazine advertising are:

a Precise targeting. With many magazines, especially trade journals or special interest magazines, segmentation and targeting can be very precise. Thus, if you have a specialized product, you can avoid wasting your money advertising to a general audience, many of whom will not be potential buyers.

b Thorough readership. An advert in a magazine will stand more chance of receiving attention than an ad placed in almost any other medium because magazines tend to be read quite thoroughly. Some special interest magazines will be read avidly by the enthusiasts who buy them, and they will usually read the adverts just as carefully as the articles.

c High quality print. Quality reproduction and the use of colour make magazines particularly suitable for products with visual appeal. When advertising in magazines this opportunity should therefore be exploited effectively.

d Long life. Some magazines are read by many people. Some are kept by subscribers as a source of reference. You can therefore receive enquiries from magazine adverts long after their original appearance.

e Overseas opportunities. Many British trade journals have an international circulation. Thus, an advert aimed at a British audience can often produce enquiries from potential customers overseas.

f Bingo cards. Many trade magazines have a reply facility known as 'bingo cards'. Each advert in the magazine will be given a number, and at the back of the magazine is a reply paid perforated card full of numbers, just like a bingo card. If the reader wants further details of any products advertised in that issue, he only has to circle the relevant numbers on the card and post it. The magazine will then send his enquiry to all appropriate advertisers. This easy reply system can make a big difference to the number of enquiries you get.

g Inserts. Many magazines offer the possibility of inserts. This means that you can have your leaflet or brochure included in the magazine. There are loose inserts or bound-in inserts. People have different experiences with the effectiveness of inserts, but for products with some degree of immediacy (for example, sale offers, events or seminars), they can be more effective than an advertisement. If you are already printing leaflets for a mailshot it can be cost-effective to print extra and use them for a magazine drop.

h Testing. Many magazines offer a split run facility enabling you to test different adverts or inserts quite easily.

The disadvantages of magazine advertising are:

a Long lead times. Many magazines have long lead times which means that you have to organize your advertising well ahead of the time you want it to appear. If you include the time necessary to arrange photography and artwork you will need to plan often up to six months ahead.

b Costs. Costs are almost always higher for magazines than for newspapers, partly because of space costs and partly because of production costs for the glossy medium. You need to decide whether the higher costs will be offset by greater effectiveness because of the advantages offered by magazines. Experimentation will provide the answer here.

The cost of magazine advertising. As with newspapers, costs vary according to circulation and space size. Examples of costs are:

Full page, black and white (add around 40 per cent for colour)

Woman's Own	£14,000
Cosmopolitan	£4230
Melody Maker	£1540
Running	£1080
Rowing Monthly	£375

Eighth of a page, black and white

Woman's Own	£1750
Cosmopolitan	£535
Melody Maker	£300
Running	£155
Rowing Monthly	£65

Cost-effectiveness. Most magazines will have a classified section, and, as with newspapers, such advertising can be very cost-effective. You need to test different sizes of ads in different positions in different magazines. And you can always increase the cost-effectiveness of your advertising by bargain hunting.

You will find that there are generally more opportunities for bargains with magazine advertising than there are for newspapers. Many magazines face intense media competition, so their advertising sales department will often be prepared to offer attractive incentives under certain circumstances.

a Discount. Much advertising space is sold at below the official or 'rate card' cost. **Always ask for a discount.** You will often get one.

b Special positions or shapes. If you can't get a discount, try to get another benefit free. You might ask for a guaranteed good position (as described in the section on positions in newspapers), or an unusual shape. If you have a diagonal or L-shaped advert it will be more difficult for the editor to fit it in with other ads, most of which are conventional full, half or quarter

Fig. 10.3 Blueprint for a successful print ad

This advertisement was voted the best business to business advertisement in 1987. It was a full page and in colour. It generated a huge number of responses. Such advertising can be emulated by companies of any size

pages. As a result, unusually shaped ads tend to be positioned with articles, further increasing their chances of being noticed.

c Remnant spaces. It is very difficult for the editors of magazines (or newspapers) to precisely fill every inch of space in their publication. As their deadline draws near they become increasingly concerned to fill any remaining, or 'remnant', spaces. As the copy date for different magazines approaches, you can try ringing them to ask if they have any remnant spaces. Of course, you will have to have all your copy and artwork ready so that you can act quickly if an attractive deal is offered. You can let magazines know that you would always be ready to fill remnant spaces at short notice. They may then come to you when they have space to fill, which puts you in an even stronger bargaining position. You would be amazed how cheaply you can sometimes obtain the space.

d Per enquiry fee. Some magazines will enter into an arrangement whereby you pay nothing for the advertising space but pay a commission on the enquiry received. Of course, the magazine will need to be confident that your advert is offering an attractive proposition, but if you feel that you have a strong case this is well worth trying.

e Soft periods. Summer and public holidays are not good times to advertise. As a result, it tends to be a buyer's market for space or time in most media during these 'soft periods'. This is when your haggling power will be at its height. Although August may not be a good time to advertise at full price, it may be highly cost-effective if you can negotiate a good discount.

f Cost sharing. Sometimes you can find another firm to share the cost of your advertising: perhaps a supplier with a much larger budget than your own. The next chapter explains how this enabled one company to afford the cost of an extensive regional TV campaign (see page 189).

Many of these opportunities for bargains apply to other advertising media as well as magazines. The most important principle is to haggle at every opportunity. If you don't ask for a bargain you will certainly not get it.

Checklist: Good print advertising

1 Have a clear, simple layout. This includes:

a an arresting photo which demonstrates the benefits offered by the product

b a headline promising a reward

c text in standard black and white set in two or more columns

d the firm's name, address, logo, etc, clearly displayed at the foot of the advertisement

e a reply slip, freephone number or other clearly identified means of response

2 Make it readable:

a speak the language of your customers (acid test – would you put it in that way if speaking with a typical customer face to face?)

b organize for easy reading, put your main points first and include sub headings

c use short sentences

d use easy words

e tell the full story – provided the layout is clear, the inclusion of plenty of text which fully explains the benefits is an advantage

3 Television. Television advertising is not beyond the means of small firms, though it will usually be cost-effective only if you have a product which will sell to a wide cross section of the community.

The advantages of TV advertising are:

a Mass communication.

b Good impact.

c Targeting. Good regional segmentation.

d Element of prestige for a small firm – 'as seen on TV'

The disadvantages of TV advertising are:

a Cost. The cost of national TV advertising is huge. Even locally, peak-time costs can be very high.

b Production. Production costs for very creative ads are extremely high.

c Wastage. For firms operating in niche markets TV is generally too broad in its coverage – you would be paying to reach a huge number of people who were not potential customers. However, if you select your TV airtime carefully you can target your market segment extremely well, for example, the slots around a gardening programme for advertising a garden centre or gardening products.

d Time. The average TV slot is 30 seconds. Firms with a small budget often have to settle for 10 second slots. Unless you have an extremely simple message this will not be enough time to say anything worthwhile.

The cost of TV advertising. Independent TV is split into fourteen regions, each run by a different company. Some cover a much higher population than others. For example, Thames TV, covering London and the South East, reaches 22 per cent of the British population. A medium sized company such as Anglia TV (East Anglia), reaches 5 per cent and a small one such as Border TV (Northern England and Southern Scotland) reaches only 1 per cent of the population, though it is important to note that in actual numbers this is over half a million people.

Each TV company sells airtime in 'commercial breaks' between and during programmes. Different advertising rates are charged at different times of day, roughly corresponding with expected audience size, with the highest prices occurring during the peak early evening viewing slots. Prices also vary considerably between regional companies, again depending on audience size. The comparisons below give some idea of the range of costs for a 30 second advertisement.

Peak-time ITV:

Thames:	£38,500
Anglia:	£10,000
Border:	£1600

Off-peak Channel 4:

Thames:	£250
Anglia:	£200
Border:	£ 35

Is TV affordable?. You could run a mini TV campaign in a small region for as little as £1000. However, unless you had a very simple message suitable for 10 second slots, it is doubtful whether such a campaign could repeat your ad sufficiently to make a worthwhile impact. Being more realistic, with a minimum of £5000 some firms could contemplate running a successful TV campaign using off-peak slots. Research has shown that off-peak slots can be more effective for the smaller advertiser than the same amount of money spent on expensive peak-time commercials. For one thing, you are less likely to be competing with the latest blockbuster coffee soap opera! If you can meet most of the following criteria TV advertising could be a worthwhile option for you.

a Target audience. You would need to make sure that your audience was well targeted with little wastage. Unless you regard a large proportion of the community as potential customers, you would need to identify a suitable TV programme which would attract an appropriate target audience.

b Discounts. It should be fairly easy to obtain a good discount on the airtime cost if you approach your regional TV company as a new local advertiser.

c Help with production costs. Most TV companies will help a new small advertiser with the production of a commercial. A very cheap 10 second visual with a basic voice-over could cost less than £500 and should be quite adequate for the small businessman. A much more professional multi-slide presentation with a more professionally produced soundtrack could be made for around £2000.

d Multiple use. You can often take advantage of the work which goes into the making of a short TV commercial by also using it to create some other company promotion. You would be part way towards producing your own company video, for example. Stills used in a TV commercial can also be used for print advertising, brochures, posters and mailshots. Cinema advertising would also be a spin-off.

e Shared cost. Suppliers may be prepared to share the cost with you if their products are visibly featured in your ad.

f Direct response. If you are experimenting with TV advertising you should always build in a response mechanism (at least into your first campaign) so that you have a clear yardstick for assessing its effectiveness. Most TV companies will help you in this respect.

g Complementary activities. Many people would argue that a 30 second TV slot (let alone a 10 or 15 second slot) is not sufficient time to sell anything. Therefore, to maximize the promotional opportunity of limited budget TV advertising you should complement it with other promotional activities. You can refer to it in your local press advertising (making the most of the 'as seen on TV' reference). You can use the same visuals or slogans in your other advertising. You could even send a video of the TV advert to your customers in case they missed it on TV!

TV in the future. As cable and satellite TV develop, lower cost air time will become more widely available, making the medium increasingly affordable for small companies. If any part of your target market is served by cable TV, for example, and your product or service has wide appeal, it would be worth making enquiries into the cost of advertising on this medium.

4 Commercial radio. At present there are 47 independent local radio

(ILR) stations. Most of the population (around 85 per cent) can receive local radio and in a typical week around 45 per cent listen to ILR at some time.

The advantages of radio advertising are:

a *Local targeting.*
b *Cheap production costs.*
c *Relatively cheap* air time.
d *A good medium* for reaching young people.
e *Help and discounts* will be available from radio stations for small first time advertisers.

The disadvantages of radio advertising are:

a *Poor impact.* Radio is often listened to as 'background' entertainment only, and so an advertisement may not receive full attention and its message not taken in.

b *Suitability.* Radio can only be used for very simple verbal messages, making the medium unsuitable for many products which depend on explanation or visual appeal.

The cost of radio advertising. Like TV stations, commercial radio stations vary widely in the size of audience they reach. Air time costs vary in proportion to audience size. In general, you can expect a 30 second local radio slot to cost around £50 to £200, although this can widely differ. For example, a peak-time slot on Capital, the largest independent local radio station, can cost over £1000, whereas an off-peak slot on a small station is likely to cost less than £10. Local radio is well worth investigating. In most parts of the country, £2000 would buy you a very respectable campaign. If you serve a local market covered by a smaller station, you could achieve an effective campaign with as little as £1000, particularly if you target your air time carefully. Local radio stations will have details of the size of their audience and the kind of people listening at different times of the day. You will tend to find that there is a high in-car audience at travel-to-work times (the time to reach men), a high housewife audience in the mornings, and a high teenage audience in the evenings, at weekends and during school holidays. It is well worth paying more to ensure that your commercials go out when the right target audience is most likely to be listening.

You will find local radio stations very helpful with the production of a commercial, but don't let them determine the tone of it. You should decide that for yourself. Listen to as many radio commercials as you can, record them and, ideally, sound out a few typical customers to see which radio commercials they like and remember. On radio it is very important to be clear and simple and avoid too much distracting background noise.

5 **Cinema.** After years of decline, cinema audiences have begun to rise again and the development of American-style out of town cinema complexes is likely to add to this recovery. Cinemas tend to have a very young audience. 76 per cent of 15 to 24 year olds claim to attend the cinema once a month, with 30 per cent paying a weekly visit. Cinema

attendance drops rapidly amongst older age groups, although certain films will draw older audiences than others.

The advantages of cinema advertising are:

a *Reproduction.* Excellent quality of sound and picture.

b *Impact.* Ideal conditions for holding the attention of the audience with the big screen and the absence of distractions. Research shows that people recall cinema commercials better than any others.

c *Targeting.* Especially good for young adults in your local area.

d *Cost.* Local cinema rates are not high. Also, the high production costs (see below) associated with producing your own advert can be avoided by using a standard advert for a certain product or service, for example, car and van hire, and adding your own company name to the advert.

The disadvantages of cinema advertising are:

a *Low audiences.*

b *Low repeat levels.* Commercials are shown only once during the evening and most people attend the cinema very infrequently.

c *High production costs.* Even if you have already done the filming for a TV commercial or a company video, the cinema contractors require two very high quality 70mm colour prints per screen, which is likely to cost at least £500.

The cost of cinema advertising. Spots can be booked at individual screens from £30 per week for a thirty second commercial. Given the high production costs, you should realistically allow £1000 for a worthwhile cinema campaign, and even this assumes that you have already shot the footage for use on TV or video. However, cinema can be extremely effective, especially if you are aiming at a young target audience.

6 Outdoor advertising. 'Outdoor' mainly refers to posters but also includes advertising on buses, taxis, railways, sports stadia, parking meters and even milk bottles.

The advantages of outdoor advertising are:

a *Targeting.* It reaches a very wide cross section of the community.

b *Impact.* Large colourful posters can have good visual appeal.

c *Use of sole attraction sites.* Some sites, for example, achieve 'sole attraction' status: people have nothing to do other than read an advert in a bus shelter whilst waiting for their bus.

The disadvantages of outdoor advertising are:

a *'Wallpaper' effect.* Most advertising experts agree that posters generally have poor impact.

b *Cost.* Printing costs for large colour posters are very high.

c *Grafitti* is a problem on some sites.

d *Long lead times.* Posters are often booked up for long periods ahead.

e *Simplicity of message.* Since most people only give outdoor adverts the most fleeting of glances, messages have to be extremely simple.

The cost of outdoor advertising. Outdoor sites are sold by a small number of contractors who each own thousands of sites around the country. They like to sell packages of several hundred sites of different sizes in various locations, but it is possible to book a small number of specific sites. As a rule of thumb you can regard £100 per month as an average cost per site, though rates vary widely according to size and location.

Largely for reasons of printing costs it would be wise for first-time poster advertisers to experiment only with the small 'four sheet' size. Such posters are 5ft × 3ft 4ins and are typically found in tube stations, bus shelters, shopping arcades, etc. Sixteen sheet posters measure 10ft × 6ft 8ins and a large 48 sheet roadside site would measure 20ft × 10ft.

In addition to the small size, you should also think very carefully about location. What kind of places do your typical customers frequent, and would they be likely to notice adverts in those places?

How do you go about buying advertising?

Unless you are going to employ an advertising agency to do it all for you (further details in the next section), you generally buy advertising time or space directly from the media owners: the newspaper proprietors, the local radio or regional TV companies, the poster site contractors, etc. If you are going to shop around effectively when buying advertising you need to be able to answer three questions:

1 Who are the media owners?
2 What does it cost to buy advertising from them?
3 What kind of an audience will my message reach through advertising in the various media?

1 Who are the media owners? The best place to find the answer to this question is *Benn's Media Directory* which costs £70 for the UK edition and £125 for the UK And International edition. It provides details and addresses of the groups/companies that own the various media, detailed information about the different types of media available and their uses, and a breakdown of some of the more technical data which the small businessman might find useful, for example, the circulation figures of magazines and newspapers, and the main social characteristics of the kind of people who subscribe to them. *Benn's Media Directory* should be available in any large library but can be obtained direct from the publishers who are:

> *Benn Business Information Services Ltd, PO Box 20, Sovereign Way, Tunbridge Wells TN9 1RQ. Tel: 0732 362666.*

2 What does it cost? The best directory for finding this information is *BRAD (British Rate and Data)*. Unlike *Benn's*, it contains all the latest media rates. It is also possible to use *BRAD* to find the media owners, although it contains less detailed information about individual media owners than you will find in *Benn's*. You should find *BRAD* in your library. If you want to subscribe, it is available at £265 from:

> *British Rate and Data, Maclean Hunter House, Chalk Lane, Cockfosters Rd, London EN4 0BU. Tel: 01 975 9759.*

3 **Who will my message reach?** All media owners produce a 'media pack' giving details of their advertising rates and the audience you can expect to reach through advertising with them. The media pack will also give booking details, such as copy dates. Media packs are a valid and accurate way of comparing different media because the advertising industry is so large and professional that various independent organizations constantly monitor the performance of different media. Media owners would therefore not get away with making false claims.

However, the details in the media pack should only be seen as a starting point. The only way to be sure which advertising media will work best for you is to experiment cautiously and monitor the results carefully. This is discussed further in Chapter 11.

Advertising agencies

Unless you are planning to spend £25,000 or over a year on advertising it is probably not worthwhile considering employing an agency. This is because advertising agencies normally get paid through commission from the media owners. In return for that commission they carry out all advertising functions free of charge for their clients. This would include audience research before the campaign, developing advertising themes and creative ideas, selecting the most appropriate media, producing adverts for those media and placing them at the times required. They normally receive 10 to 15 per cent commission on the cost of all the advertising space or time they book on behalf of their clients. So, the commission on your advertising spend of less than £25,000 will not make you a lucrative account for most advertising agencies. You would therefore not get their best people working on your account and the agency would not be prepared to devote very much time to it. Alternatively they would want to charge a fee over and above the commission they were receiving. If you use an agency for non-advertising activities, such as brochures or mailshots (agencies refer to such work as 'below the line') you will be charged a straight fee. In this case always secure a detailed quotation for the work to be carried out before you go ahead.

If you are keen to try an advertising agency you should shop around for a local one. Unless you liaise closely with an agency you cannot expect good advertising, therefore you must choose one within easy reach. You will find details of advertising agencies in *Benn's Media Directory* and in the *Advertisers Annual*, which also lists agencies' main clients, and what they specialize in. However, it is more appropriate for most small firms to look in the local *Yellow Pages*, pick out several local agencies and make contact. You should state honestly how much you are prepared to spend, explain why you would like to use an agency and find out what kind of fee they would charge. Then, choose between those you can afford by asking them to produce some rough ideas for an ad for you to evaluate (many agencies will do this on spec even for small firms), and choose the agency which seems to have the best ideas. If you are a small advertiser, many agencies will be reluctant to do any work for nothing. In this case they will show you work they have done for other companies, and you can always approach those clients to gain their view of the agency's effectiveness.

Finally, if you do decide to opt for an agency, try them out with a small assignment initially and evaluate the result thoroughly before committing yourself on a larger scale.

When should you use advertising?

The greater the number of customers in your target market, the more cost-effective advertising will be. If you have less than 1000 potential customers in your target market it is most likely that other methods of promotion will prove more cost-effective than advertising. Between 1000 and 10,000 potential customers, advertising becomes more useful, but not necessarily the most effective way of reaching your target audience. Once there are considerably over 10,000 in your target audience, other forms of promotion find it much more difficult to compete with print advertising. As the numbers rise further, other forms of advertising media such as local radio, posters and TV will become viable options.

Checklist: Advertising

1 Audience size. It is most unlikely that advertising will be the most cost-effective form of promotion for your company unless your target market contains several thousand potential customers.

2 Choosing the right media. Getting your message to the right audience is more important than coming up with a clever advert. You must therefore be prepared to devote time to careful selection of the right media. Even in markets with large numbers of customers, media fragmentation may make it very difficult to reach a reasonable proportion of your target audience on a small budget. Unless you know that there is a particular medium (for example, a specific magazine) which reaches your market, it would be wise to carry out some simple research to identify your customers' sources of information. Alternatively, experiment to find out which media produce the best response to your advertisement.

3 Simple messages. Adverts should be clear and concise, whether display or classified. Have a clear relevant headline and, in larger display ads use a photo.

4 Advertisement size. In general, for small firms, many small ads will prove more cost-effective than a small number of large, expensive adverts.

5 Response. Always make it easy for people to respond to your ads. Have a coupon with a freepost address, or a freefone telephone number, or better still, use a magazine which makes it easy for readers to respond via a bingo card.

6 Test and monitor. Always test the content of your ads, if only informally with a few friendly customers, before running them. You should also monitor the response from all ads, since this data will provide evidence on questions such as the best size, shape, positioning and media for advertising your product.

7 Negotiate. All media will have a rate card but much print space and air time is sold at below rate card costs. Discounts are frequently available from TV, local radio and some magazines for new advertisers. They may

also give you help with the production of your advertisement. You can also get some good bargains if you are prepared to book your space or air time at the last minute, when the media owners will be more than pleased to fill their remnant space at almost any price.

Effective direct mail

What is direct mail and when should you use it?

Direct mail is personal communication between yourself and an individual member of your target audience. The communication takes place through an envelope rather than over the telephone or face to face. However, you must always remember that it is personal communication and so it is vital to follow the golden rule of designing your mailshots as though you were speaking with your customer face to face.

Direct mail has seen enormous growth in recent years. It has shown itself to be an extremely cost-effective form of communication, particularly in medium sized target markets (100 to 20,000 potential customers). You can use direct mail whatever the size of your target audience, but if it grows much above 20,000 you will need to consider segmenting it if only because of the handling difficulties you will encounter. Mailshots involving tens of thousands of letters will be processed more efficiently by a mailing house with mechanical stuffing, wrapping and sorting facilities.

The advantages of direct mail are:

a Cost. Direct mail is very suitable for firms with budgets of all sizes. It is possible to run very successful direct mail campaigns on low budgets.

b Segmentation. Mailshots can be targeted specifically at your desired audience. You can divide the market into as many segments as you want and alter the message, offer, timing or other details to suit the different needs of different segments. If you serve a small niche market you can eliminate the waste associated with many other forms of promotion.

c Controllable. Unlike many other forms of promotion you can remain in control of all stages of a mailshot.

d Evaluation. Since you know exactly how many mailshots you send out, it is easy to monitor the cost-effectiveness of direct mail, provided you keep a careful check on the number of responses coming back. It is also easy to test different direct mail methods until you come up with a successful formula.

e Impact. If it is carefully designed, direct mail can overcome the problems of poor impact often associated with junk mail.

The disadvantages of direct mail are:

a Junk mail. Contrary to what many people think the problem with direct mail is not the negative reaction to the volume of mailshots received by the average individual at home or at work. Although the volume is growing research studies have shown that despite complaining about receiving mailshots, most people still glance at all those they receive and read some quite carefully. The problem is the fact that much of the direct mail that people do receive is of no interest or relevance to them. To overcome this your mailshots must be carefully designed to appeal to your target audience.

b Management time. The most important single aspect of successful direct mail is getting your message to the right audience in the first place. As seen below this is an extremely time-consuming task if it is to be done properly. As well as the compilation and maintenance of a mailing list, the organization involved in sending out mailshots, particularly if you are working to a deadline, can be immense.

Managing mailshots

1 **Personalization**. Unless you personalize your mailshots you are throwing away the medium's biggest advantage.

2 **The mailing list**. If you are going to address mailshots to named individuals, you need a detailed and accurate mailing list. This is the most important aspect of any mailshot. A poorly targeted or out of date list will restrict your response rate. A business to business mailing list can become out of date at the rate of a third of its entries per annum.

There are two ways of obtaining a mailing list. You can buy one or you can develop your own.

a Buying
Bought-in business lists. There are two problems with bought-in lists: cost and effectiveness.

Firstly, cost. Lists vary in price but as a rule of thumb a bought-in list will cost you £50 to £100 per 1000 names. Thus, you have to add up to £1000 to the cost of a mailshot to an audience of 10,000. This is aggravated by the fact that the price quoted is for *renting* a list, which gives you a once-only chance of using those names. If people respond, you can put those names on your own database and use them again, but the non-responders you can only use once. Thus, the cost of renting a mailing list would arise for every mailshot. However, you can *buy* lists giving you permanent ownership and the cost would be roughly double that of renting.

Secondly, effectiveness. Bought-in lists will almost always be less effective than your own because they tend to suffer from lack of relevance and, often, they will not be up to date. However, if you do not have your own database and you are in a hurry, you will have to rent or buy an external list. There are many suppliers:

IBIS Information Services, Waterside, Lowbell Lane, London Colney, St. Albans AL2 1DX. Tel: 0727 25209.

Market Location, 1 Warwick St, Leamington Spa CV32 5LW. Tel: 0926 34235.

Morgan Grampian Direct Mail Service, 30 Calderwood St, London SE18 6QH. Tel: 01 855 7777.

Reed Database, Quadrant House, The Quadrant, Sutton SM2 5AS. Tel: 01 661 3355.

Bought-in consumer lists. Companies offering consumer lists tend to start with the electoral register as a comprehensive source of names and addresses. They then proceed to segment people according to two main criteria:

'You are where you live'. Known technically as 'geodemographics', these consumer lists allow you to target specific markets based on very precise post code districts. The assumption is that people living in larger detached houses on new estates will tend to share similar lifestyles and make similar purchases and that their lifestyles and buying behaviour will tend to show clear differences from those of people living in smaller, terraced urban housing. Lists which enable you to target consumer mailshots in this way include ACORN, MOSAIC and Pin Point.

'You are what you do'. Known technically as 'psychographics', this kind of database segments people according to the kind of things they have spent their money on. Relevant data is usually gathered from questionnaires accompanying product guarantee cards or placed in magazines. The theory is simple. Someone who has bought a large petrol driven lawnmower is likely to have a larger than average garden and a larger than average income making him (or her) a good prospect for similar upmarket gardening products. If you are selling very specialized products or services this type of database is almost certain to offer you the most effective way of targeting new potential customers. Examples of such lists include Lifestyle, Behaviourbank and Facts of Living.

The best way to find out more about such databases is to contact one or more of the following companies:

ACORN, CACI Ltd, 59-62 High Holborn, London WC1V 6DX. Tel: 01 404 8034.

MOSAIC, CCN Systems, Talbot House, Talbot St, Nottingham NG1 5HF. Tel: 0602 410888.

Pin Point, Pin Point Analysis Ltd, Mercury House, 117 Waterloo Rd, London SE1 8UL. Tel: 01 928 1874.

Lifestyle, Lifestyle Selector, 36 Broadway, London SW1H 0BH. Tel: 01 222 7404.

Behaviourbank, BRICODA Ltd, Teddington House, Broad St, Teddington TW11 8QZ. Tel: 01 943 5511.

Facts of Living, 4th Floor, Petersham House, 57a Hatton Garden, London EC1N 8JD. Tel: 01 831 1888.

Due to the growth of direct mail in recent years, there are a very large number of companies now involved in providing lists and other direct mail services, such as creative services, printing services, and mechanical handling services. The best general source of reference for other list providers and direct mail services in general is *Benn's Direct Marketing Directory*, available for £75 from:

Benn Business Information Services Ltd, PO Box 20, Sovereign Way, Tunbridge Wells TN9 1RQ. Tel: 0732 362666.

b Your own database

The best form of mailing list is your own up-to-date database which perfectly matches your target market, thus eliminating wastage. If you can make repeat sales (or first time sales of other items) to past customers, then your customer database is a vital mailing list. However, most firms will need to go beyond that and compile a prospects database of potential customers with whom they have not yet done business. To develop your own prospects database you need to go through the following steps:

Step 1: Determine method of storage. The more business direct mail could bring you the more you should be prepared to invest in compiling and updating your own mailing list. If you have a large number of potential customers, and/or each customer is potentially worth a lot of business, it will be worth investing resources in your own database. On the other hand if you have a small target audience you can manage very efficiently with a card index box system. You simply put the details of your prospects on the front (see Chapter 5), and use the reverse side to record all dealings with them, including mailshots sent, telephone follow-ups, sales visits and so on.

As far as computerization is concerned, the minimum investment required would be around £1500. For this you could buy a hard disk IBM compatible computer such as an Amstrad PC 1512. You would need a 'hard disk drive', but a black and white monitor is perfectly adequate. You then need a good database software package such as Ashton Tate's 'dBase III' which you can programme without much difficulty to your own exact requirements. It is possible to buy off-the-peg software for mailing lists, which would be easier in the short term, but in the long run, if you expand and want to store increasing amounts of information you would benefit from the greater flexibility of a more general software package like dBase III.

Step 2: Determine record format. If you are using a computer you will have to specify which categories of information you want your individual customer records to hold (see pages 57 and 58). The biggest mistake you are likely to make at the outset is to make insufficient provision for the amount of information you will want to record in the future. If in doubt, include more rather than less categories of information on each record – you can always leave some of them blank.

Step 3: Compile list. You then need to decide where to get your names from. You will already have some contacts which you could put straight into your database but you will also need to find a lot more names and addresses of potential customers. You could start off by buying some lists, consulting *Benn's Direct Marketing Directory* to identify the most appropriate sources. Alternatively you can key in your own names and addresses using published directories. You could use the kind of large national directories recommended in Chapter 5 as the basis of a business to business mailing list. They are all broken down into different types of company. The main problem here is that everybody else uses the same directories, so you might find some additional names by using local sources. There are a surprising number of local business directories, whose entries often contain more detailed information than the large national directories.

The best way of finding local directories is to consult the reference sections of libraries in large towns (details in Chapter 5). Of course, the most detailed, readily available source of names and addresses is the telephone directory.

Step 4: Updating the list. The chances are you will want more information about the prospects on your list than you can get from most directories. You also have the problem of keeping it up-to-date. The best way to tackle both of these problems is to operate a system whereby you telephone all the names on your database, ideally at least once every two years. This enables you to fill in missing details, update yourself on changes, and qualify prospects: ask a few simple questions to ascertain whether or not they are likely buyers of your product, for example. For many products, such as replacement windows, it is essential to sift out unlikely buyers. For products of more general appeal you can get away with a more blanket coverage. *NB* Prospects considered unlikely buyers should be left on your database but marked in such a way that the computer will not mail them. In two years' time things may be different. They may have become excellent prospects.

Step 5: Purging. You do need to purge your mailing list of 'dead' names. The best way to do this is to have your name printed on the outside of all mailshot envelopes. The Post Office will then return to you free of charge all letters that it cannot deliver, usually because the recipient has 'gone away'.

Step 6: Registration. If you store information about other people on a computer you need to register under the Data Protection Act. It costs £22 and is only a formality, but if you store a mailing list on a computer and it contains the names of individuals, you are breaking the law if you do not register. Application forms are available from post offices or direct from:

The Data Protection Registrar, Springfield House, Water Lane, Wilmslow SK9 5AX. Tel: 0625 53577.

As you can see, your own database can represent a huge investment. The thing to do is take it step by step. Start off with a manual system. If mailshots generate profitable business go a step further and computerize. If all continues to go well, expand your database, then start updating it. But do remember that database management activities are very time-consuming. Once you are committed to direct mail you will probably need to employ someone to be responsible for compiling and updating your database. If you are short of space this is a task which is ideally suited to freelance operators. Many people like to work part-time from home and equipped with a low cost computer and a telephone, this is a job that can be easily done in this way.

However, always remember that compiling and updating your own mailing list will never be cheap. If you were to employ someone part-time to be responsible for this task it would cost you around £5000 per annum. If you use a freelancer you could pay by results, for example, ten pence for each company telephoned and entered on the database or five pence for each company entered from a directory. On this basis the compilation of your own database would cost £100 per 1000 entries, plus telephone calls, plus the cost of acquiring directories or lists to enter. If you update your list every two years, the additional costs would be around £100 per 1000 entries plus telephone costs.

3 Design of mailshots. A brochure stuffed in an envelope and sent to 1000 prospective customers does not constitute a mailshot. To work well, the material needs to be carefully designed to maximize the advantages and minimize the disadvantages of direct mail. There are a number of specific points to consider in this respect.

a Impact. A mailshot has a very short length of time in which to grab the interest of the recipient before it is discarded. If you have the budget and the potential sales are high enough, you can virtually guarantee to buy the attention of the target audience in the way shown by Mitsubishi on page 158, or, less reliably, by offering a substantial prize, as shown in the case study of Naylor Clayware on page 176. Alternatively, and on a much lower budget, you can try and grab the attention of the recipients by clearly identifying the subject matter as something which will interest them, as shown in the case study on the next page.

However, many mailshots will be sent out in large numbers with the objective of appealing to only a small proportion of recipients. A one per cent response will often be a perfectly satisfactory rate of reply for such a mailshot. The material in fig. 10.4, advertising an industrial seminar, is a typical example.

Fig. 10.4 A mailshot (front only)

By far the most important aspect of this mailshot is the phrase 'industrial marketing', in bold letters at the top of the leaflet. This will catch the attention of people for whom the seminar is relevant at that particular time and should give them a reason to read further.

b Copy. It used to be considered that a good mailshot had to be one which included a long, intimate letter. In recent years, however, it has become increasingly accepted that clear, simple messages which are quick and easy to read and demonstrate their relevance instantly to the target audience, are usually the most effective.

Joddymix: getting the message across

The Joddymix mailshot followed all the rules of relevance, simplicity and brevity, and was one of the main factors which helped that company to overcome the problems explained in Chapter 1. Having decided that direct mail was going to offer the most cost-effective way of reaching its target market, Joddymix decided to invest in its own database from the outset. There were three sources of names for the database:

1 The *Yellow Pages*, with a relevantly targeted section (plastering contractors), formed the basis of the database. Entries were telephoned to find out company size and names of relevant individuals. The criteria for their inclusion on the database was their weekly consumption of plaster: if they used under twenty bags a week they were considered unlikely prospects for the Joddymix machine and were therefore not taken into account.

2 There also existed potential customers outside of the plastering segment, for example, builders, public sector direct works and machine hire firms. Press releases were used to generate their interest in the machine and responses to them were placed on the database.

3 Distributors, with their wide connections and experience, were also helpful in supplying names for the database. However, since the Joddymix mailshot provided them with leads, it was in their interests to do so.

The mailing leaflet was obtained from a company called Interprint. An A5 four sided folded leaflet with two colour photos and printed on good quality matt art paper, the mailer cost less than £500 for 5000 copies. This included the cost of the preprinted reply cards, which were affixed to the mailer with a small spot of glue in one corner.

The mailshots were sent out in waves as there was no point in generating leads faster than they could be realistically followed up by sales visits or supplied with the product. Response rates consistently approached 20 per cent, which was extremely good in that kind of target market. Moreover, the mailer presented the benefits so clearly and simply that many respondents took little, if any, persuasion to purchase.

c Letter. Notice that the Joddymix mailshot did not include a letter. The envelope was personally addressed but there was only the leaflet inside. Some people argue strongly that there should always be a long personalized letter, stressing all the benefits that you offer. However, in business to business markets you ought to minimize the number of items in the envelope. The recipient should be able to open the envelope and realize instantly what the subject of the mailshot is. Reading a letter takes time.

ARE YOU STILL DOING THIS??

The Way of the Future!

★ **WORK**
Joddymix gets through a lot of work. Run continuously, it will mix 260 bags of Browning in a 40 hour week. Joddymix doesn't get tired in the afternoon, or go off sick.

★ **PRODUCTIVITY**
Joddymix eliminates the need for labourers, enabling skilled men to devote their time and energy to putting plaster on the walls. This has enabled firms using Joddymix to increase productivity by up to 50%.

★ **JOB COMPLETION**
Improved productivity allows completion ahead of schedule and avoids the risk of penalty clauses.

★ **ONE COAT PLASTER**
In addition to all backing plasters, Joddymix is recommended for use with one coat plaster. In fact, it will produce one ton of mixed plaster per hour.

★ **CONSISTENCY**
With Joddymix, the consistency and quality of the mix never vary. A simple mixture stiffness setting ensures a perfect mix for all types of plaster.

★ **EASE OF USE**
Joddymix will function under normal building site conditions. It requires only a 110 volt single phase power supply and does not need mains water. It is portable and self-cleaning.

SPOT THE DIFFERENCES
This mixer fetches its own water from the tub, eliminates dust and mess, and produces a more workable mix than you've ever used. With the Joddymix taking care of the mixing, the men can devote all their time to putting plaster on the walls, making full use of their skills and not wasting time fetching, carrying and mixing.

THE WAY OF THE FUTURE

How many bricklayers do you see without a cement mixer?

Before long, the same will apply to plastering. Ask anybody who already uses a Joddymix.

"I wouldn't ever consider working without a Joddymix now."
(David Potter, Oldham. Self employed plasterer.)

"Joddymix enables me to do as much work as two men who have to mix by hand, and the quality of the mix is so much better."
(Alan Morrison, Telling North Western)

To find out more about Joddymix, return the prepaid card now!

Please send me more information on the Joddymix JM 6/70 Continuous Plaster Mixer.

Name

Address

Postcode

Fig. 10.5 The Joddymix mailshot

An exception, however, is when you are mailing to regular customers. In this case, as with anyone you know well, politeness demands a letter.

d Envelope. For most mailshots, especially to business markets, it is preferable to use a plain envelope. You will need to print your firm's address on the outside so that you will get any returns. Some firms, however, plaster the outside of the envelope with information and offers, but for many mailshots this can be counterproductive. In so blatantly advertising themselves as a mailshot some will be consigned to the bin unopened. There are two possible exceptions to this rule. Firstly, if you are running a competition and are offering a very attractive prize, it may be worth drawing attention to it on the envelope. Secondly, if you are mailing hobbyists who are very likely to be interested in your product, it may pay to draw recipients' attention to them on the envelope. If you are going to use the envelope for a message you should test it initially. Send half your mailshots with the message on the envelopes and half without and compare the results.

If you are including a personalized letter you should use window envelopes, otherwise the task of matching up letters and envelopes is too time-consuming and risky. If there is no personalized letter involved, use sticky labels for the address and white envelopes. Rented mailing lists can be supplied on sticky labels for a small extra charge.

e Response mechanism. If you want replies you must make it as easy as possible for people to respond. As well as reply paid cards, you should consider free of charge phone numbers, credit card facilities if orders are expected, and facilities for replying or booking by fax.

British Telecom and the Post Office both have local sales offices (details in the telephone directory) who will be pleased to give you information about freefone and freepost services. You pay a small standing charge for such services but then pay per response. These facilities almost invariably prove cost-effective in consumer markets. In business to business markets, however, their benefits are more debatable, and their absence will probably not reduce your response by much.

4 Administration. There is a lot of administration even in a relatively small mailshot. Leaflets have to be designed and printed well ahead, envelopes ordered, mailing lists ordered (or sticky labels printed and stuck onto the envelopes). Envelopes have to be stuffed, with great care if personalized letters are involved or if a number of different mailers are going out together. You should allow at least three months to organize a mailshot from beginning to end, including the printing of leaflets, and one month from receipt of all stationery to the time you send it out. Unless you have very large numbers (over 25 000) you will find that mechanical handling facilities are expensive. Why not recruit others to stuff your letters in return for payment? Many firms use scouts, school children, pensioners and other forms of low cost labour to stuff mailshots.

As far as postage is concerned, there is a Post Office scheme called Mailsort which offers a discount provided you bundle your letters in separate sacks for each post code (although this is extremely time-consuming). Although you can qualify for Mailsort with a mailshot as small as 4000 it is normally not worth the small saving on postage unless you are mailing well in excess of 10 000 leaflets and you have a computer programme which prints off address labels in post code order. For more details on Mailsort write to:

The Royal Mail, Freepost, Phoenix Way, Cirencester GL7 9BR.

Also available from the same address are two free booklets: *First-time users guide to direct mail,* and *Refining your direct mail strategy.*

5 Following up. Some mailshots, such as in fig. 10.4, do not require following up. Large numbers are sent out, and if only a one per cent response (in the form of bookings) is achieved, the promotion will be considered a success. Follow-up would therefore not be cost-effective. Many mailshots, however, are not expected to generate sales directly. They will stimulate enquiries which need to be followed up. You must, therefore, have your next steps fully planned. For instance, you may send product brochures, followed by a telephone call, followed by a personal visit. With some mailshots, to relatively small audiences, it often pays to follow up all recipients by telephone regardless of whether or not they have responded.

The cost of mailshots

The cost depends very much on what you put inside the envelope and on additional costs such as prizes given away in free draws. You should also remember overheads such as the cost of compiling and updating your own database. However, assuming a relatively modest leaflet in the envelope and a rented mailing list, the figures below represent a good guide to the costs of a 5000 mailshot.

	£
Postage @ 15p	750.00
Envelopes @ 2p	100.00
Leaflets (*printing*)	500.00
Leaflets (*photography*)	250.00
Stuffing @ 2p	100.00
List rental @ £75 per 1000 names	375.00
Total cost	2075.00

Non-personalized door to door mailshots to local households could considerably reduce those costs. Distribution would be around £30 per 1000, you would eliminate the list rental and you could eliminate the envelopes and stuffing. However, door to door is generally much less effective than personalized direct mail.

Response to the mailshot

It is impossible to predict the response that a particular company might get to a mailshot. However, in very general terms, experienced practitioners would agree that the following response groupings can be taken as a guide:

> Door to door household leaflets: 0.2% to 1%
>
> Postal direct mail
>> Cold consumer lists: up to 2%
>> Cold business to business lists: up to 4%
>> Warm consumer lists: up to 7%
>> Warm business to business lists: up to 15%

A 'warm' list is defined as one which is made up of good prospects who are likely buyers of the product you sell. Of course, much better response rates can be achieved with an excellent product or service presented in the right way. On the other hand, with a badly targeted list, with a poor leaflet or the wrong product it is possible to end up with disastrous response rates.

Mitsubishi Electric (UK): an example of a mailshot

In 1985 Mitsubishi Electric (UK) decided to tackle the British air circuit breaker market seriously. Six companies were recognized suppliers, but none dominated. Mitsubishi's sales stood at 280,000, a very small percentage of this 4.5 million growth market, but they aimed to take 15 per cent of the market by 1987 and 20 per cent by 1990.

Mitsubishi knew that although they had the advantage of a recognized company name, it was not associated with this product. So their objectives were as follows:

1 To make all significant users of air circuit breakers aware of the Mitsubishi source of supply.

2 To increase their product knowledge (although as the company was already well-known it was the reliability of the Mitsubishi product that was really the only factor of any relevance here).

3 To help potential buyers comprehend the benefits of buying from Mitsubishi, particularly its high levels of customer service, possibly the chief differentiating factor in this market.

4 To generate enquiries which the sales staff would hope to convert into trial orders.

To achieve their objectives the company had to command the attention of its prospective customers and it began this process on December 2nd when a list of 300 panel builders, not normally potential buyers of Mitsubishi air circuit breakers, received a lumpy Jiffy bag. Inside was a red tape measure, (overprinted with the Mitsubishi name and logo) attached to a white card bearing the question 'How do your circuit breakers measure up to Mitsubishi?' By the time the recipients had grappled with the securely affixed gift they were bound to have read and decoded the simple message that Mitsubishi supply air circuit breakers.

Over the next few weeks the three hundred recipients received another four mailshots of this nature, each containing a new message and gift:

Screwdriver – 'How not to screw up your reputation with
customers!'
Scissors – 'Practical ways to cut your circuit breaker costs'.
Torch – 'Are you still in the dark about the world's most
reliable air circuit breakers?'
Pen – 'The final word in power protection'.

Each parcel followed a consistent format of containing red gifts overprinted with the company's logo and name on a stiff white card with the headline in bold black capitals. Under the headline was a short paragraph with a few additional details and at the foot of each mailer was a perforated reply paid card inviting recipients to ask for more information, attend a demonstration or request a copy of the manual.

Even after the fifth mailshot very few cards had been returned! However, the twelve-strong sales force was to follow up each individual recipient in his territory soon after their receipt of the final mailshot. As soon as they began the task it became clear that despite the lack of unpromoted reponse Mitsubishi had made a very favourable impression on the target audience. This was shown in two ways. Firstly it was easy to make appointments with virtually all mailshot recipients and secondly, once face to face, they found prospects already interested in the product, resulting in a marked improvement in the order to sales call ratio.

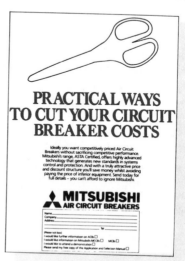

Fig. 10.6 Mitsubishi mailshot

Mitsubishi marketing staff were convinced that the bulk of the communications work was done by the sequential mailshot to the three hundred known users of air circuit breakers, which is certainly where most of the orders came from. And orders were won. By 1987 they had not only surpassed the 15 per cent share target but attained the 1990 goal of 20 per cent, representing sales of over one million. To turn £20 000 of marketing money into sales gains in excess of £750 000 is not a bad performance!

The detailed cost breakdown of the five step sequential mailshot were as follows:

	£
300 tape measures	502.00
300 screwdrivers	488.60
300 pairs of scissors	488.00
300 torches	605.00
300 pens	128.80
Artwork	1 000.00
1500 Jiffy bags	750.00
Stuffing and postage	850.00
Total cost	4 812.40

This example provides a number of important lessons:

1 By including the gifts with the mailshots the problem of making an impact was overcome. In effect Mitsubishi bought its prospects' attention.

2 The gifts, together with the repetitive nature of the mailshot, overcame the threat of recipients forgetting the company and the product it was offering.

3 For a virtually unknown supplier in that market, the company's objectives of generating awareness and knowledge were appropriate and achievable.

4 The messages were very short and simple and were consistent with the objectives.

5 The audience for the sequential mailshot was very well targeted.

6 The sales force was used to follow up the non-personal communications, concentrating on the area of the persuasive aspects of the promotional task.

7 The free gifts did increase audience participation – they would have felt they had received 'a good deal' out of the exercise.

8 Above all it shows that real communications successes are possible despite all the problems of information overload and on a small budget – provided the campaign is well planned.

Checklist: Direct mail

1 Targeting. Direct mail is at its most cost-effective when used to target precise market segments.

2 Personalization. It is the only medium which offers the possibility of mass personalized communication. Never miss an opportunity to personalize your direct mail.

3 Organization. Careful advanced planning is essential in direct mail campaigns.

4 Database. The most important factor in the success of a mailshot is accurate targeting, which means using the right mailing list. If you compile and update your own database it is always likely to be more relevant to your market than an outside list.

5 New customers. Bought or rented lists can be a cost-effective way of reaching new customers, especially in specialized consumer markets.

6 Impact. A novel idea can make a huge difference to the impact made by your mailshot.

7 Clarity. Simple clear messages are required on mailshot leaflets to ensure that the recipients can grasp its subject even if they only glance at it for a split second.

8 Response. Always ensure that mailshots have a clear response mechanism. Use the freepost or freefone reply services, especially in consumer markets.

Public relations

What is PR?

Public relations (PR) include any activities designed to improve mutual understanding between your company and its target audience. Such activities may include open days at your factory, seminars on relevant technical matters, a regular company newsletter, information or technical guides, and so on. Some of the activities the small businessman could consider are outlined in the next section.

Some PR activities

1 Press releases. The most common, and often the most cost-effective PR activity is sending out press releases. Costing only your time and perhaps some black and white photographs, press releases can be very successful in generating enquiries.

There are a few simple guidelines to follow for press releases:

a Media list. Compile a list of all media which may be interested in your message. Details of specialist magazines, segmented into different markets, can be found in *Benn's Media Directory*. If you feel that your press release will have a particularly wide appeal you should send it to the Press Association who may distribute it to national newspapers, television and radio. The address is:

The Press Association, 85 Fleet St, London EC4P 4BE. Tel: 01 353 7440.

b Clarity. Editors are very busy. It is vital therefore that your press release follows a recognizable format and its message is understandable and easy to assimilate. You should give a clear but simple identification heading at the top of your release, with your own company name, address and telephone number at the end of the text. Use short sentences and paragraphs and use double spaced typing, on one side of the paper only. If suitable, attach a small black and white photograph.

c Summary paragraph. Many magazines will not print your whole press release. Moreover, rather than rewrite it in a more concise format, they may simply print part of it, chopping paragraphs from the end upwards. Therefore, your first paragraph should include a summary of all the essential points you wish to communicate and you should position your more important detailed points as close as possible to the beginning of the release.

d Objectivity. To get the best out of press releases or other PR activities, information should be presented in an objective manner, designed to educate or build relationships rather than to persuade.

Always bear in mind the fact that newspapers and magazines, are often heavily dependent on press releases as a source of stories. Therefore, you have nothing to lose and everything to gain by distributing your press release as widely as possible.

An example of how a press release appeared in print is shown on page 163. Joddymix Ltd sent out a 300 word press release accompanied by a 7″ × 7″ black and white photo to all the suitable trade journals listed in *Benn's Media Directory* – 44 in total. In the event, only nine of those

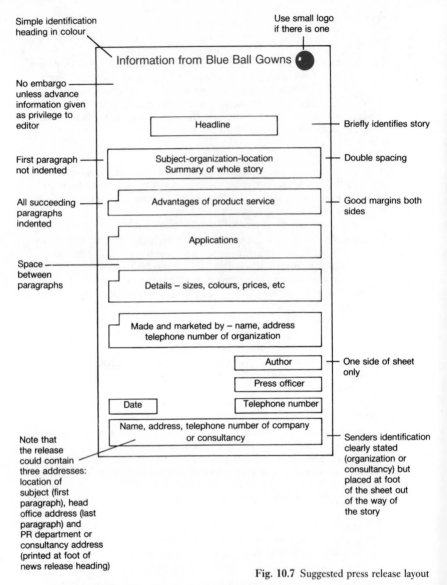

Simple identification heading in colour

Use small logo if there is one

Information from Blue Ball Gowns

No embargo unless advance information given as privilege to editor

Headline — Briefly identifies story

First paragraph not indented

Subject-organization-location
Summary of whole story — Double spacing

All succeeding paragraphs indented

Advantages of product service — Good margins both sides

Applications

Space between paragraphs

Details – sizes, colours, prices, etc

Made and marketed by – name, address telephone number of organization

Author — One side of sheet only

Press officer

Date

Telephone number

Name, address, telephone number of company or consultancy

Senders identification clearly stated (organization or consultancy) but placed at foot of the sheet out of the way of the story

Note that the release could contain three addresses: location of subject (first paragraph), head office address (last paragraph) and PR department or consultancy address (printed at foot of news release heading)

Fig. 10.7 Suggested press release layout

magazines actually printed the Joddymix information, usually in summarized form. However, over 200 valuable sales leads were generated from this press release.

2 Signed articles. This is the term used for a two or three page (usually technical) article, often accompanied by an advertisement for the firm, which is printed in a magazine. The authorship is accredited to the

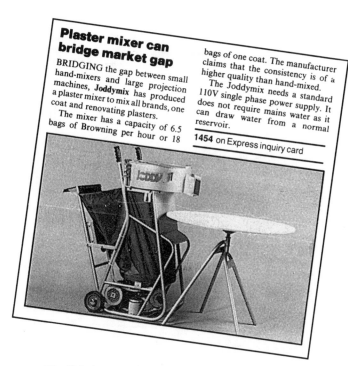

Plaster mixer can bridge market gap

BRIDGING the gap between small hand-mixers and large projection machines, **Joddymix** has produced a plaster mixer to mix all brands, one coat and renovating plasters.

The mixer has a capacity of 6.5 bags of Browning per hour or 18 bags of one coat. The manufacturer claims that the consistency is of a higher quality than hand-mixed.

The Joddymix needs a standard 110V single phase power supply. It does not require mains water as it can draw water from a normal reservoir.

1454 on Express inquiry card

Fig. 10.8 A result of the Joddymix press release
From *What's New in Building*, May 1989

individual and his company. Signed articles are a very good way of improving your firm's image in specialist markets. If you think you could produce an interesting technical article you should write to a suitable magazine giving the editor full details of your idea.

3 Technical guides. A step beyond the signed article would be the production of a technical guide or explanatory booklet about your product or service. To be successful as a PR mechanism, however, the guide must be of some interest or educational value to your potential customers.

Let's use as an example a technical guide produced by Flowguard Ltd, a company specializing in pumps and pipework. The 40 page technical guide covered topics of interest to organizations making extensive use of pumps and pipework. 1000 copies of the guide were printed with an attractive, glossy, two colour cover, at around 50p per copy. The text was published by an agency at a cost of 1p per page, giving a total cost of less than £1.00 per copy for a very professional end result, as shown in fig. 10.9. Subsequent press releases, announcing the publication of the technical guide (see fig. 10.10 for example), produced over 500 enquiries.

4 Customer newsletter. As a way of keeping in touch with past customers or good prospects, reminding them of your company's products

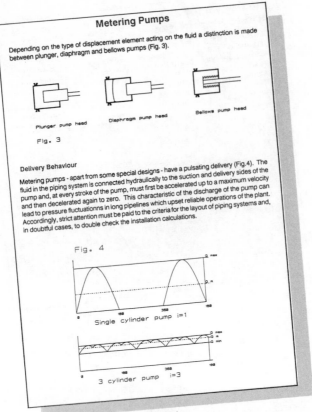

Metering Pumps

Depending on the type of displacement element acting on the fluid a distinction is made between plunger, diaphragm and bellows pumps (Fig. 3).

Plunger pump head Diaphragm pump head Bellows pump head

Fig. 3

Delivery Behaviour

Metering pumps - apart from some special designs - have a pulsating delivery (Fig.4). The fluid in the piping system is connected hydraulically to the suction and delivery sides of the pump and, at every stroke of the pump, must first be accelerated up to a maximum velocity and then decelerated again to zero. This characteristic of the discharge of the pump can lead to pressure fluctuationns in long pipelines which upset reliable operations of the plant. Accordingly, strict attention must be paid to the criteria for the layout of piping systems and, in doubtful cases, to double check the installation calculations.

Fig. 4

Single cylinder pump i=1

3 cylinder pump i=3

Fig. 10.9 Sample page from Flowguard Ltd technical guide

A COMPREHENSIVE guide to dealing with noise and vibration in pipelines and pumping systems is now available free from pulsation damper specialists **Flowguard Ltd**. Contents include information on the causes and effects of pulsations and pressure surges, methods of elimination in both discharge and suction pipework and extensive data on damper selection.

CIRCLE Reader Enquiry No 245

Fig. 10.10 A press release announcing the Flowguard Ltd technical guide

and promoting an image of good customer service, a regular newsletter can be very effective.

Holmen Chemicals: customer newsletter

Holmen Chemicals supplies additives for the animal feedstuffs industry and employs only ten people in the UK. On a very small budget it has maximized its promotional effectiveness through a very well managed PR campaign. For over ten years the firm has sent a quarterly newsletter to customers, which is written in-house, photocopied onto plain paper without photographs, but is full of information which is both interesting and useful to the target audience.

Printing and mailing of the 2000 copies sent out each quarter costs about £500. The objective of the newsletter is to continually reinforce, in the eyes of customers, Holmen's image of technical expertise and good service.

5 Customer clubs. Similar in purpose to customer newsletters, a 'club' atmosphere can further boost customer loyalty. They are particularly suited to children's products or hobby products.

6 Open days. You do not have to have impressive premises full of machines to host a successful open day. An open day is just a good excuse to gather people together in order to further your key PR objective – developing mutual understanding. For example, celebrating the fifth anniversary of your company's formation would be a perfectly adequate reason to hold an open day. Make sure there are plenty of refreshments available and as many people as possible representing your company to circulate with the guests.

7 Hospitality. If your customers are far flung you may need to give them a better incentive to socialize with you. Many firms invite important customers to sporting events. Again, plenty of refreshments are provided and there is plenty of time to develop good relations. You must remember that the main purpose of PR events is to develop understanding, not to sell. Many customers will be offended if you try to use hospitality invitations as a cover for selling, but anything you can do to improve relationships will help your selling efforts at a later date.

8 Sponsorship. Sponsoring events is a very common PR activity. Many well known companies sponsor prestigious events, especially sporting events. However, they do not just do it for the thrill. They do it because they see it is a very cost-effective way of reaching the large audiences they want to reach. Small firms considering sponsorship as a promotional activity (rather than a charitable donation), should enter into deals on exactly the same basis. You should satisfy yourself that through the sponsorship arrangement you will reach your desired target audience, and, moreover, reach it in a more cost-effective way than you could if you spent the equivalent sum of money on alternative forms of promotion.

Checklist: Effective PR

1 The function of PR. PR should not be used to sell. It should be seen as a way of educating customers or developing your company's reputation.

2 The value of press releases. Press releases are an extremely cost-effective form of promotion for small firms. You should send them out at every opportunity and distribute them as widely as possible.

3 Time-consuming. PR activities are usually very time-consuming, but are not usually very costly in cash terms. This makes PR especially appropriate for small firms with more time than money to invest.

Brochures

The purpose of brochures

There are very few firms that can operate in a professional manner without some kind of literature. It serves four main purposes:

1 **Enhancing your company's image.** Whether it is a brochure on your company, leaflets or data sheets on your products or an extensive catalogue, customers will generally expect to see some kind of literature. This is particularly true when small firms are selling to larger organizations. Informative, well produced literature will boost your company's image no end, poor or no literature will certainly be detrimental to your business.

2 **Saving time.** For new contacts who want to know something about your business it saves you, or your staff, having to repeat the same information over and over again.

3 **Permanent record.** There are often good reasons for communicating information verbally to your customers, but unfortunately people's memories tend to be rather short. Without a permanent record of your company and its products potential customers will often forget it. A brochure, on the other hand, will often be stored away and retrieved when the need arises.

4 **Evaluation of alternatives.** Brochures enable customers to evaluate alternative products. Some people prefer to make their own choice rather than feeling that they are being 'sold to'. In such circumstances your brochure must do the selling job for you. It must, therefore, compare very favourably with your competitors' literature.

What makes a good brochure?

Different kinds of literature are appropriate to specific situations, but there are some general guidelines which you should follow.

1 **Quality.** Always go for the best quality you can afford. Important brochures should be on good quality paper and include photographs where relevant. It is better to have a small number of high quality leaflets than a large collection of rather tatty ones.

2 **Photographs.** Good photographs are often crucial in the overall impression created by a brochure. Always have them taken by a good, professional photographer. Choose him carefully. Ask to see some examples of his work before you commit yourself. A good photographer may have slightly higher fees, but they are worth paying because he will be able to make even the most uninspiring product look more interesting.

3 Design. The rules are very similar to those for a good print advertisement (see page 140).

Checklist: Good brochure layout

1 Simplicity Have a clear layout which is easy to follow.

2 Photographs. Use photographs wherever possible. Make sure photos are of a high quality, display the product very clearly and are in colour if cost allows.

3 Simple wording. Make headings and sub-headings tell the story. Use short sentences and simple words and avoid jargon.

4 Diagrams. Put complex information into visual form (charts, diagrams, photos) whenever possible. Visuals are much easier to take in than long tracts of text.

5 Benefits. Don't just describe the features of your product – sell the benefits. Remember, your brochure often has to do your selling for you, therefore it should describe your product in terms of what it will do for the customer.

4 Branding. Brand continuously. For example, the brand name 'Joddymix' appears prominently four times in the single-sided leaflet in figure 10.11.

Fig. 10.11 A good example of a low cost but very effective brochure

5 Data sheets. Some customers do like to receive large amounts of information which they evaluate carefully before making a decision. You should always provide information in such a way that it is available but does not clutter up your brochure. For technical products data sheets can be used to convey detailed information. Typed, word processed or desk top published sheets photocopied cleanly, will usually be quite adequate. The brochure shown in fig. 10.11 was accompanied by four pages of photocopied data sheets which included diagrams, for potential customers requiring more detailed technical information.

6 Paper. Avoid lightweight paper which always gives an impression of cheapness and saves you very little money. A good matt art finish will often create a much more up-market image than the more traditional glossy finish, and not at that much more cost.

Costs

The most cost-effective form of obtaining colour brochures is to use a printer offering a standard package at a very competitive rate. You will find many such printers advertising in the business to business classified advertising sections of a newspaper like *The Sunday Times*.

The leaflets in fig. 10.5 and 10.11 were printed by a company called Interprint and firms like Interprint can offer attractive prices through standardizing their production rather than reducing the quality of the finished article. Some of the larger printers offer a very wide range of formats from which you can choose but if you require literature which does not conform to those formats all the cost advantages of standardization would be lost, and you would be charged significantly more. It is also worth noting that if you are in a hurry these sorts of firms offer a special 'rapid' service, although at extra cost. For special printing requirements it would be better to use a small local printer.

The standard international paper sizes are:

A5 $8\frac{1}{4}'' \times 5\frac{7}{8}''$
A4 $8\frac{1}{4}'' \times 11\frac{3}{4}''$
A3 $11\frac{3}{4}'' \times 16\frac{1}{2}''$
A2 $16\frac{1}{2}'' \times 23\frac{1}{2}''$

Desk top publishing

A fairly recent innovation, desk top publishing has brought professional publishing techniques within the reach of many firms. DTP systems allow you to lay out text and produce diagrams on a computer screen. A laser printer enables them to be printed crisply and professionally. Complex designs (of the kind shown in fig. 10.12) can be produced with ease once the operator has mastered the computer programme.

A complete system, comprising computer, software and a laser printer would cost in the region of £4000–£5000. If you already have a suitable hard disk micro computer, the cost would fall to £2500–£3000. If you produce a lot of black and white literature, customer newsletters, product instruction sheets, and so on, a desk top publishing system would almost

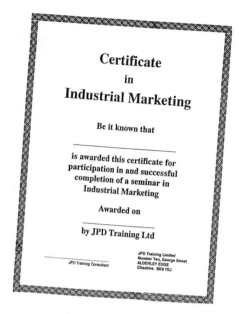

Fig. 10.12 Produced in minutes by desk top publishing

certainly be a good long-term investment. If you have occasional requirements, many firms now offer a desk top publishing service, charging around £10–£15 per A4 page.

Exhibitions

When to use exhibitions

Exhibitions are ideal for demonstrating product benefits and for meeting new customers. They are therefore more useful if you sell 'enthusiast' products such as boats or working products such as machines, rather than inanimate products such as timber or services. They are also likely to be more cost-effective in new markets, especially overseas markets where you would expect to meet many new people, than in existing markets where you would tend to spend much time talking with regular customers (who will remain customers whether or not you attend the exhibition). Some exhibitions, such as the Boat Show, can represent excellent opportunities to make sales or take orders.

Exhibition planning

More than any other promotional activity, exhibitions require meticulous advance planning, starting several months before the event itself. The use of a schedule planner on a spreadsheet or a wallchart (as shown in fig. 6.6), is essential if you are to coordinate, on time, the many tasks that result in a successful exhibition. All the following tasks should be scheduled.

1 **Identifying suitable exhibitions.** There are over 3000 specialist exhibitions in the United Kingdom alone, and many more overseas. Some are huge events with an international reputation, held at leading venues such as the National Exhibition Centre near Birmingham. Others, by comparison, are relatively small regional events. The main source of information about forthcoming exhibitions is the *Exhibition Bulletin* which is available from:

Exhibition Bulletin, London Bureau, 266 Kirkdale, Sydenham, London SE26 4RZ. Tel: 01 778 2288.

Published monthly, an annual subscription to the *Bulletin* would cost around £40. However, unless you plan to visit or show at a number of exhibitions, a trip to the library would be more sensible. A good commercial library should also stock *Showman's Directory*. Costing below £10, *Showman's Directory* specializes in agricultural and rural events. It includes events such as steam rallies and horse shows, which are often good opportunities for gaining low cost local exposure. This publication can be obtained from:

Showman's Directory, Brook House, Mint St, Godalming GU7 1HE.

You should be looking at these reference sources as far ahead as possible – ideally over a year before you want to exhibit. If possible you should also visit a show and have a good look around the year before you intend to exhibit for the first time.

2 **Selecting the right show.** In many cases an advance visit will not be possible, particularly since many major trade exhibitions are not held every year (many are biennial). You may therefore have to evaluate possible exhibitions without having seen them. If so, the crucial question to ask yourself is: 'is the proposed exhibition a good way of reaching my target audience?' Exhibition organizers publish statistics of the previous year's attendance (exhibitors and visitors). These should be thoroughly scrutinized, and you could contact a couple of previous exhibitors to ask their opinions and experiences of the show. However, if you are in doubt about the exhibition's appropriateness for your target market you should carry out a simple telephone survey (as outlined in Chapter 5), to determine what proportion of your target audience usually attends such an exhibition.

3 **Budgeting.** Exhibitions tend to be extremely expensive. You should prepare a full list of direct and indirect costs (such as travel, subsistence, management time before, during and after the event) and compare this total cost with the alternative promotional initiatives which could be mounted with that sum of money. Consumer exhibitions, such as the Boat Show or the Ideal Home Exhibition, where products are sold as well as being exhibited will usually more than pay for themselves. However, trade exhibitions are more of a promotional than a selling activity and their value must be compared with other promotional activities such as advertising or direct mail.

4 **Booking space.** If you can afford it, and you expect it to be cost-effective you need to go ahead and book stand space. It will often be

necessary to book months ahead. Moreover, space at some exhibitions will be oversubscribed and the previous year's exhibitors will be given first option to re-book their space. In such cases you can do no more than put your name on the waiting list, but you are not guaranteed a space. For oversubscribed exhibitions you should accept any space offered, however small or unsuitable, in order to get on the list of exhibitors. Once you have found a way in, you will find it much easier to negotiate better space the following year. Do remember that you will have to pay a significant deposit on booking, and the balance up to three months before the show. Exhibitions are not good news for your cash flow!

5 Stand design. If you do exhibit you must do it well. You will be in a shop window with many of your competitors affording customers an ideal opportunity to compare rival suppliers. You should therefore take the largest space you can afford because the other costs will soon dwarf the cost of the space itself. If your stand is spacious, it will be much easier to make it look attractive. A shoddy, cluttered or confusing stand could do some harm to your competitive position in the marketplace. Display panels should be professionally designed and produced, photography should be excellent and the manufacture and preparation of display products should be scheduled well ahead of the exhibition. Needless to say, your display products should be immaculate.

At most exhibitions, the organizers offer 'shell stands'. They are like a small office with panels forming three sides and, usually, a roof. They have an open front, or, with a corner site, two open sides. Shell space is not cheap, but if you do not have exhibition panels of your own it is extremely convenient. You need only worry about your display material to go on the panels and your own exhibits.

If shell stands are not available, you will have to design your own, but it is possible to buy or rent panels. If you look in the *Yellow Pages* under 'exhibition stand contractors', and 'display contractors' you will find many local suppliers. Unless you are going to exhibit frequently, hiring would be better than buying. Panels bought for one exhibition may not remain suitable if your stand size or shape changes in subsequent years. To hire or buy, exhibition panels are very expensive. If you have the skills to make your own you could save a lot of money, but be warned: nothing looks worse than a tatty, home-made stand.

When designing your stand or planning your exhibits, you must always read the organizer's regulations very carefully. Many are very strict about what is and isn't allowed. You may be limited on power points (and will almost certainly pay a high fee for use of each one). There may be height and weight restrictions. You may have to submit details of a self-designed stand to the organizers by a certain date for their prior approval. It is also important to note that some organizers will not allow you to carry out your own electrical or joinery work in the hall but have to use their contractors. Check the regulations beforehand.

Finally, you should have a dummy run where you erect the stand and set up the fittings and main exhibits. This serves two important purposes. Firstly, it ensures that you avoid the biggest danger –trying to cram too much in. If it looks cluttered, remove some items. You will attract more visitors to your stand if there is some space for them! Secondly, the dummy run ensures that your stand and display equipment do actually work.

6 Stand management. You should ensure that you have enough people to man your stand. Exhibitions are very tiring and staff should be allowed frequent breaks. It is all too clear to visitors when stand personnel are visibly wilting. If your firm does not employ many people, see if you can involve some relatives or friends. They may not be able to answer technical questions but there are many other tasks at an exhibition which they could help you out with.

All staff need to be thoroughly trained as far as the objectives, customer contact and recording procedures are concerned. As for any promotional activities you need to have clear objectives for the exhibition. For some large consumer type exhibitions you may simply want to maximize daily sales. Other objectives could include launching a new product or meeting new potential customers, distributors or overseas agents/partners. You may have PR objectives, creating a certain kind of image or developing relationships with existing customers whom you don't often meet face to face. There will be so many things to do at an exhibition that your staff need clear objectives to focus them on the most important tasks.

Presentation is critical. Stand staff need to be immaculately presented, with appropriate dress and clear identification badges. Stands can easily degenerate into an untidy mess as the day proceeds, therefore attention must be paid to 'housekeeping'. In order to ensure that all the elements of effective stand management are adhered to, someone should be made personally responsible for stand management.

7 Attracting visitors. Large exhibitions are bewildering places. Although there are programmes available with diagrams showing where all the stands are, most visitors (apart from maybe one or two stands that they have to visit for a predetermined purpose) simply wander around, drifting into those stands which attract their attention. There is no doubt that at a crowded exhibition many stands will fail to make a lasting impact on the visitor. So you have to decide what you are going to do to make visitors **notice** and **remember** your stand.

Firstly, the stand layout must be clear enough to communicate immediately to passers-by the product or service your company is promoting. However, it has a short amount of time to communicate its relevance to the target audience. If you have done your market research and you know what customers see as the main benefits of your product or service you should highlight those. You should also make sure that your exhibits, photographs and headers on display panels are clearly visible from a distance of at least 10 yards. As with advertising and direct mail, ensuring that your stand projects a clear message is the most important factor for attracting the attention of an appropriate target audience. For example, if your small business is in the line of offering maintenance service to industry you will want to attract the maintenance managers, who may make up, say, only 20 per cent of the total audience. In this case, employing gimmicks to attract all and sundry onto your stand will simply involve a lot of work and cost for relatively little reward. There is also a danger that some of the maintenance managers may notice the gimmick, but simply dismiss it and pass by your stand, having failed to appreciate its relevance to them.

Sometimes, you will see a very high percentage of the target audience as potential customers. In this case you have to consider the best way to attract large numbers onto your stand. Communicating a clear message from your stand is still the most important single factor, but you may want to consider some gimmicks to attract additional visitors. A popular one is a free prize draw which visitors enter by placing their business card in a box. This has the additional advantage of helping you to build up a mailing list. The prizes should be aimed at individuals rather than businesses. Another idea is to offer ice cool drinks–water is quite adequate. At stuffy, crowded exhibitions, the offer of an ice cool glass of water is extremely tempting for many people. However, remember that the visitor attracted by this sort of gimmick will almost certainly be of less long-term value to your company than those attracted by the relevance of your message to them.

8 Records. Exhibitions are about meeting people. You should take details of all the people you meet. Asking people to put their business cards in a box as an entry to a prize draw is useful because it saves the time of writing down their details. Even more importantly, new contacts who express a serious interest in your products should be kept on record with a view to following them up as soon as possible after the exhibition. It is vital that you have a system which ensures that the names of all visitors are recorded.

9 Other promotional activities. There are many other promotional activities which can be coordinated with the exhibition, some of which should be given a higher priority than others. The most important is literature. It is top priority to have impressive up-to-date literature on your stand. The brochure may often be the only memory of your company and its stand that many visitors will take away. The design and printing of brochures must be planned well ahead. Some firms leave it to the last minute and actually turn up at the exhibition without their new literature, promising lamely to send it on!

The exhibition programme is important–at least your stand entry is. Those people who are going to be methodical about their visit to the exhibition will read the stand entries. Make sure yours is clear and simple and communicates benefits for your customers rather than blowing your company's own trumpet. Advertising in the exhibition programme should come much further down your list of priorities: that money would be better spent on your literature or your stand. The same holds true for advertising your attendance at the exhibition in magazines. If you advertise regularly, include a small caption in your ad which mentions your attendance at the exhibition but use the bulk of your space to advertise your product, not the exhibition. Most magazines devote much editorial space to a relevant exhibition. A press release about the attractions on your stand will prove very cost-effective.

One final promotional activity that you could coordinate with an exhibition is a mailshot to existing customers and important prospects inviting them to your stand and giving them a good reason for making the visit. This has the dual advantage of reaching your target audience and of being inexpensive.

10 Evaluation. Since exhibitions are so expensive it is essential that a cost benefit post mortem is carried out. The numbers of visitors to the stand and new contacts made are important criteria, but efforts must be made to monitor orders won during and subsequent to the exhibition if a realistic evaluation is to be made.

Exhibition costs

All professional exhibiting is expensive. Attending certain exhibitions can be extremely expensive. Therefore, you must budget accurately beforehand so you know exactly how much the venture will cost, and then tightly control your costs against budget as you get ready for and actually attend the event.

You should budget for the following categories of cost:

a *Stand space.* At least £1000 for a small stand at any reasonable event.

b *Stand design.* Whether you have a shell stand or not you will still need display materials such as display panels, photos, models, banners, lettering and sample products. You may need to buy or hire a modular stand, a reception desk or lighting equipment. For first-time exhibitors the cost of filling your stand space with suitable display materials will almost certainly exceed the cost of the space itself.

c *Extras.* Electrical sockets, telephones, shell stand roof and carpet tiles are amongst the items that can appear as extras on costs.

d *Travel.* For yourself, your staff and your equipment.

e *Accommodation.* Meals and overnight accommodation can be very expensive, especially in London and close to the National Exhibition Centre in Birmingham. It is worth buying one of the many publications now on sale which give details and prices of low cost accommodation in Britain. Most of these are priced between £5.00 to £7.00 and are available in most bookshops.

f *Time.* How many people will miss how many days' work to prepare, assemble, man, tidy up and follow up your exhibition? If you attach an opportunity cost to that time (what other things could you achieve with that time) it helps to put into perspective the true cost to your company of attending the exhibition.

Checklist: Attending exhibitions

1 Planning. You need to think well ahead to identify suitable exhibitions and to plan your activities for those you wish to attend.

2 Audience. A good exhibition is one that will enable you to reach a significant number of people from your target audience.

3 Stands. Unless you are already equipped with exhibition display equipment, a shell stand scheme will be best. If you can only rent the bare space, hire rather than buy display panels initially.

4 Regulations. Read the organizer's regulations very carefully, otherwise you may get some nasty surprises.

5 Manning. Adequate manning is essential, which means enough people, properly trained and well presented.

6 Projecting the right image. The two critical objectives are projecting a clear image to appeal to relevant prospects in the audience, and doing it professionally. Unprofessional looking home-made stands should be avoided at all costs.

7 Records. One of the main reasons for exhibition attendance is to extend your list of contacts and prospects. Thorough recording of stand visitors' details is therefore essential.

8 Opportunity cost. The full cost of attending an exhibition must be projected. Before committing yourself to attend consider whether that time and money could achieve more for you if invested in other promotional activities.

Sales promotions

What are sales promotions?

Sales promotions should be seen as additional incentives to buy. They include money off, an extra product free, giveaways, competitions, merchandising (special displays and in-store promotions), tokens to collect, complementary offers and many more short-term incentives designed to tempt the buyer into committing himself to the purchase. Though sales promotions are mainly used in consumer markets they can be very successful in business to business markets, particularly if they are used to give people an incentive to respond rather than to place an order.

The cost-effectiveness of sales promotions

Giving additional incentives is bound to cost money, either in the form of a giveaway (be it a gift or a prize) or in the form of a reduced price. Sales promotion therefore eats into margins and, as emphasized in Chapter 9, it is difficult to recover, through additional sales volume, any margin that is given away to buyers. You should therefore approach any sales promotion ideas very cautiously and must convince yourself that you stand a good chance of ending up in pocket. The following points are particularly important:

1 Short term. Sales promotions usually have a relatively short-term effect. Although they may give people a short-term motive to act, they do not usually contribute to the building of long-term loyalty.

2 Costs. A sales promotion must be sufficiently attractive to consumers if it is to be effective. However, added attraction means higher costs. You need to consider very carefully whether you can realistically expect to recoup those costs through higher sales.

3 No 'freebies'. In today's highly competitive business world there is no justification for simply giving away products: all such sales promotions must have clear objectives.

Naylor Clayware: an incentive to respond

Naylor Clayware had the objective of promoting a new range of clay
drainage pipes to the building industry, a fragmented market containing
thousands of small firms in addition to the well known giants. It has
always been notoriously difficult to gain a response in such markets,
particularly for a product which is perceived as 'old tech' and therefore
unlikely to offer any worthwhile new developments. Therefore, to attract
attention to its campaign, Naylor Clayware decided to offer a £14,000
Land Rover as the first prize in a free prize draw. An extensive advertising
campaign in the trade press highlighted the opportunity to win the Land
Rover and included an entry coupon for the draw. Direct mail was used to
send a free draw entry form to all 26,000 registered NHBC builders and
point of sale display material, including free draw entry forms, was
supplied to all builders merchants stocking Naylor products. Following a
four month campaign, almost 10,000 entries had been received at a cost of
around £7.50 per response.

A breakdown of the cost of each promotional medium revealed the
following:

Costs (excluding Landrover)	£
Advertising, space and production	46,400
Mailshot	9550
Merchandising	5600

Responses	
Advertising	3846
Mailshot	3340
Merchandising	2291

Cost per reponse	£
Advertising	12.06
Mailshot	2.86
Merchandising	2.44

Since the prize draw was open to anyone (they have to be, by law), not
all entrants were potential customers. An examination of the responses
produced 4000 qualified leads (average cost £18.75 per qualified lead).
The quality of the advertising leads was very poor. The response from the
merchants was better, but still included many non-customer groups such
as painters and decorators. Not surprisingly, due to the more selective
nature of the medium, a higher proportion of the direct mail responses
became qualified leads. Further promotional activity was concentrated on
the 4000 qualified leads and by the end of the year the company's sales
target for the product had been met.

As far as sales promotion is concerned, this study shows how it can be
used very profitably to give customers an additional incentive to respond.
Having obtained their response and established their interest other
promotional methods can be used to move them further towards a
purchase.

Telephone selling

As the costs of personal selling grow, telephone selling is becoming
increasingly popular. The telephone can be used at many stages of the
marketing process, including research, generating new business via
prospecting or following up responses to other promotional initiatives,
selling and post-purchase customer service. Firms can employ their own

telephone staff in-house or may prefer to use the services of a specialist telesales company. However, the small businessman using the external agency must ensure that he is billed in terms of contacts made. Fees should be less than £10 per contact made, which, considering the number of attempts one sometimes has to make to get through to a suitable person, and the high cost of daytime calls, can be very cost-effective, especially if high value products are involved.

Key points to bear in mind about telephone selling are:

1 Pre-call research. The names of prospects, their position in the organization, their own firm's business, and, ideally, their likely level of interest in the product or service will all help to make calls more effective.

2 Script. All calls should have an objective, and a script which will work towards that objective. If necessary, the script can be modified in the light of experience as the calls are made.

3 Communication is two-way. Never talk at the customer. Involve him in the conversation as early as possible through appropriate questions.

4 Keep records. Complete a simple record form giving brief company details, time of call, type of respondent plus the result of each call, and, most importantly, details of any action resulting from the call. For 'warm' prospects a recall date shoud be set. Over a period of time this data will provide information about the best time of day to call, the best kind of person to speak to and, if records are sufficiently detailed, the best script to use.

5 Customer service. Don't overlook the valuable and cost-effective role the telephone can play in reminding customers that you care about them. You should have a planned schedule for calling regular customers simply to ensure that they remain happy with your products and service.

Personal selling

The importance of personal selling

Many companies do not sell but sit and wait for business to come to them. It is almost certainly one of the most serious mistakes that can be made. Some markets, such as mail order and self-service supermarkets, operate with very little personal selling, but most firms are involved in markets where personal contact is a critical factor in the final stages of guiding customers towards a purchase.

Sales training

Selling is a professional skill that can be learned. Anybody in your company who ever gets involved in selling face to face or on the telephone should be sent on a professional selling course. To find out about good selling courses in your locality you should contact your local Training Agency area office, whose addresses and telephone numbers can be found in your telephone directory or by consulting the companion volume in this series *Starting a Small Business*. In particular, subsidized sales training may be available locally under the Agency's 'Business Growth Training' scheme.

Principles of selling

Generally speaking, sales of most products tend to follow a broadly similar pattern. This takes the form of seven main steps:

1 Ask questions
2 Present your solution
3 Overcome objections
4 Reassure the prospect
5 Close the sale
6 Sell the extras
7 Follow through

To get the most out of this section you should be thoroughly familiar with the principles already covered in Chapter 3. If you don't understand the principles of buyer behaviour you will find it hard to make yourself a good sales person.

Step 1: Ask questions. Good sales people ask questions and listen, so that they can understand their prospect's needs, problems and priorities. Bad sales people jump in with their prepared presentation. No limit should be set for this 'probing' stage of the selling process. The longer it goes on the better. The more you understand your prospect the more effectively you will be able to sell to him.

Experience will tell you the kind of questions which work best for you at this stage. In many business to business sales it is advisable to begin with broad questions about the prospect's company, its products and his role within that organization. If he offers to show you round that gives you even more opportunity to get to know him and his company. If the prospect has an existing supplier you need to ask questions about his current buying behaviour. What does his firm use the product for? Is the current supplier satisfactory in terms of product, delivery, service, etc? What does he pay? For a new product or service that the prospect is not already buying you need to explore the reasons behind his firm's interest in making such a purchase. You should also try to get some information about other people influencing the purchase: who are they, what will their roles and priorities be?

For retail sales the questioning will be more direct. You will ask what the prospect is interested in, what sizes, colours, models, types – anything to get the prospect talking. Your objective in Step 1 is to find out the kind of things which will make the prospect want to purchase a product or service that you can supply.

Step 2: Present your solution. Having questioned the prospect you should have some signposts to guide your presentation. Your objective during Step 2 is to **match** your offering with the needs and desires of your prospect. Successful sales people do not make long presentations covering every conceivable benefit offered by their product or service. They carefully select and highlight those benefits which they think will be of most interest to the prospect. If necessary they throw in more questions during the presentation stage.

When making the presentation it is essential to talk in terms of benefits rather than features. Don't tell prospects what the product or service is, tell them what it will do for them. The fact that a product is made from stainless steel is a feature. The fact that it will not go rusty is a benefit – and of much more interest to the average buyer. Your objective is to present matching benefits: benefits which meet your customer's needs or solve his problem.

Step 3: Overcome objections. As you make your presentation and ask more questions to make sure you are still on the right lines, you will probably uncover objections or reservations on the part of the prospect. Professional handling of these objections will make a significant contribution to your success rate in making sales.

Firstly, it is important to note that if you are meeting a lot of objections the fault probably lies in your own selling technique during Steps 1 and 2. Trying to rush the sale rather than spending time to understand the prospect and match your benefits with his needs is usually the main problem. However, even the best sales people have to handle some objections. They tend to come in three varieties: genuine objections, misunderstandings, and excuses.

Some objections are based on genuine areas of mismatch. Some sales conversations reach a stage where it becomes quite clear that the benefits offered by a product or service do not really meet the customer's needs. If this occurs you should be totally frank, admit it and do two things. Firstly, you help the prospect, if possible, to solve his problem elsewhere, perhaps by directing him to a more suitable product made by another company. In the long run this will gain you a friend who will speak well of your business to others. If you persuade someone to buy something unsuitable you will gain an enemy who will tell everyone about your attitude to customers. Secondly, you learn from the experience. Coming across lots of customers with needs that you can't meet can be the start of a new marketing project!

Many objections are based on misunderstandings. This might be down to a lack of real communication but you should also be aware that very often prospects will not come straight out with their real objections. Therefore, to try and eliminate misunderstanding, it is always a good idea to begin by asking the prospect to clarify the objection. Many objections, even about the price, can be handled with ease once you have isolated the specific point that is worrying the prospect. By going over the main points again, and asking one or two more questions in areas where the prospect seems doubtful, it is often possible to clear up misunderstandings.

The third kind of objection, the excuse, is not really an objection at all. It results from the natural fear most people have of making the wrong decision. This leads people to try to defer difficult decisions. Some firms try to overcome this type of objection by offering the prospect a good incentive to commit himself, for example, a free maintenance contract with all machines ordered by such a date. However, before giving anything away you should try to overcome excuses by moving into Step 4 of the seven step sale plan.

Step 4: Reassure the prospect. When you have offered a package of benefits which genuinely meets the prospect's needs and he is still reluctant to commit himself to the purchase he needs reassurance that he is in fact making the best possible decision. It is for this stage of the sale that you should save evidence about the popularity or success of the product or service in question. A fashion item may be a bestseller or some sports equipment may have been used recently to win a major championship. Even better, a product or service may have received a favourable review in a magazine such as *Which?* Don't waste these gems of information at the beginning of your presentation, save them until Step 4 to reassure the wavering prospect and clinch the argument.

As stressed in Chapter 3, buying decisions are rarely made by one individual in total isolation in consumer or industrial markets. You should always be aware of the fact that your wavering prospect will probably have to justify his purchase decision to his wife, his boss, his friends or his fellow directors. If your questioning during Step 1 was carried out professionally you should have a good idea who is lurking in the back of the prospect's mind as he agonises over the decision. Try to bring the silent influencer out into the open. For industrial purchases stress benefits that your prospect can sell to his colleagues or superiors. Your objective is to remove any doubts the prospect may have over the consequences of committing himself to the purchase. He wants to buy it, but wants to be able to justify his decision.

Step 5: Close the sale. Sooner or later you have to ask the prospect to commit himself to the purchase. Choosing the right time to close the sale is something that comes with experience, but there are some well tried closing techniques which will help. First of all you should be satisfied in your own mind that you have successfully handled the prospect's objections. Ask yourself:

1 Did I understand the real objection?
2 Did I ask it back?
3 Did I solve the problem?
4 Did the prospect agree that I solved it?

If you passed all these tests you should be seeing a change in the prospect's behaviour signalling that he is preparing to commit himself. Prospects become more relaxed and friendly, less defensive or critical. They may start asking specific questions, such as: 'did you say there was a choice of six colours?' Even better they may start asking questions which hint that they may be interested in placing an order, such as: 'are they available off-the-shelf?', or: 'what kind of polish do you recommend for these shoes?'. If you start getting signals like this it is time to ask for the order.

Some selling courses and books, especially American ones, will produce a long list of 'unbeatable' closing techniques. In reality, it is not the closing technique itself but the preceding discussion which will determine your ability to win the order. If you have done a professional job and convinced the prospect, they will now be ready to buy, so just ask for the order in a straightforward way: 'would you like to place your order now sir?'. If you have prepared the ground properly you will not get many rejections at this point. However, you should remember that in complex sales, especially with customers representing large organizations, you will often not get to this point in one visit. It can take several sales calls to move all the way through the selling process.

Step 6: Sell the extras. In many cases selling the extras is very important to a firm's profitability. Some companies, for example, make more money out of spares and maintenance contracts than they make from the sale of the original equipment. Electrical equipment needs batteries or a plug, cameras need films and shoes need polish. If you don't have any extras to sell, perhaps you should think of some. Having made the big decision to buy the major item, what's in the odd extra? You will never get easier sales than selling the extras.

Step 7: Follow through. Having closed the sale and sold the extras you now face your biggest and most likely mistake. You breathe a big sigh of relief and zoom off in search of your next prospect. But what about the prospect you have just been working on, often for several weeks? Having just invested all that time to turn prospects into customers, now is not the time to start neglecting them. Never forget that your best prospects are your existing customers. Look after them and they will buy again, and recommend you to others. Your objective in Step 7, therefore, is to ensure that your new customer becomes a totally satisfied one, for example, is he aware of the guarantee form and procedure? If you have industrial customers, don't just pass the order on to the works or your sub-contractor and then forget about it. Note the delivery date or any special arrangements in your diary and ensure that they are all accomplished. You are the customer's contact point. It is with you that the customer will develop a relationship which hopefuly gives him confidence to buy again.

Organization for selling

To sell successfully you have to be well versed in selling techniques and well organized. The following simple points will help to improve the effectiveness of your company's selling efforts.

1 Clear objectives. Everyone involved in the selling must have clear objectives. For example, which products are to be sold to what kind of customers in which areas? This helps people to target their efforts in the most appropriate way. They should also have targets to strive for, and be rewarded with a bonus if they meet those targets.

If you are too small to employ a salesforce, someone must have clear responsibility for the selling activity, even if this only accounts for a proportion of their time. That person should be set specific selling ojectives and his performance should be evaluated against those objectives.

2 Training. Salesmen are made rather than born. Even the most naturally gifted salesperson will benefit enormously from professional sales training. You should have a plan which ensures that everyone involved in selling in your company receives training on a regular basis.

3 Sales presentations. Firms should invest in their salesman's 'toolkit' as well as his training. Good quality presentation folders, perhaps a video or other demonstration aids, and possibly even a lap top computer to work out technical data on the spot, can all enhance the salesman's image, performance and give him an edge over the competition. Sales presentations should also be thoroughly prepared and rehearsed in-house to give the salesperson added confidence.

4 Efficiency. On average, salespeople spend only one sixth of their time selling. The remainder of the time is accounted for mainly by travelling and administrative duties. Journey planning is essential to minimize costs and maximize selling time, and the firm should also consider how it can minimize the administration load of salespeople. For example, sales staff should not have to spend time generating or qualifying leads. This should be done for them by advertising, mailshots, telesales or other promotional techniques which are handled by office-based staff. Field sales staff should be given 'warm' leads with only the date and time of the appointment to be fixed.

5 Morale. Selling is not an easy job. It can be very lonely and it is easy to swing from the excitement of success to the despair of failure. Salespeople have to face rejection more than virtually any other profession. Firms should therefore make a positive effort to maintain the morale of sales staff through regular meetings at which problems can be discussed; through frequent contact, if only by telephone, to avoid the feeling of isolation; and through an understanding of the importance of their role within the company.

6 Records. Although administration should be minimized, records must be kept if the performance of the salesforce is to be monitored. Using one of the off-the-shelf salesforce record systems (such as Kalamazoo), which are available from business stationers, form-filling time can be kept to a realistic minimum. A formal record keeping system also helps firms to keep control of their absentee workers. Without proper records, how do you know whether your sales staff are working 40 or only 20 hours per week?

Summary

1 All communication is difficult but marketing communications are particularly difficult because of the remoteness of the audience and the level of competition for its attention.

2 There are many different kinds of promotional activity. It is only through careful experimentation that you will discover which techniques work best for you.

3 Whatever promotional techniques you do employ, make sure you execute them professionally. Quality photographs, clear leaflets, impressive exhibition stands and professional sales presentations will pay dividends. Cheap looking, unprofessional promotional activities will do more harm than good. **If in doubt, do less, better.**

Action

1 Do you advertise? If so, how much do you spend on each advertising medium that you use, and how much does it cost for each enquiry or new customer you win? Is your advertising cost-effective? Are all the media you use paying for themselves? If there is any doubt, could you use that money to better effect on other promotional activities?

2 Do you keep your customers' names and addresses on a proper customer database? If not, start one this month. It is one of the most worthwhile promotional measures you can take. Unless you sell once in a lifetime purchases, your past customers are your best prospects.

3 Do you send out at least six press releases per annum? If not, write one this month. Write one about your most recent new product or your best-selling line. Consult *Benn's Media Directory* and send your release out to as many editors as possible.

4 Has anybody in your company undergone professional sales training? If not, contact your Training Agency area office immediately to find details of suitable courses—you may qualify for subsidized training.

11 Planning promotional campaigns

Aims of this chapter

Chapter 10 examined the main ways businesses get their messages across to potential customers. But, why do firms do all these things? What, exactly, do they hope to achieve? And how do *you* ensure that the money spent on promotion is wisely invested rather than wasted? This chapter will attempt to answer these questions by looking at:

- The importance of your audience
- How to plan your promotional campaign
- How to decide what to spend your money on
- How to get the best out of specific activities

Understanding your audience

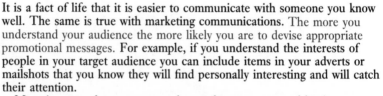

It is a fact of life that it is easier to communicate with someone you know well. The same is true with marketing communications. The more you understand your audience the more likely you are to devise appropriate promotional messages. For example, if you understand the interests of people in your target audience you can include items in your adverts or mailshots that you know they will find personally interesting and will catch their attention.

More importantly, you must understand your customers' buying behaviour. For example, for a fax machine seller, the advert for an audience which is familiar with the product and its uses and sees the purchase as a 'mechanical' buy would be very different from an advert for an audience which knew very little of fax machines and regarded their purchase as a 'problem' buy.

So in order to develop appropriate promotional messages you need a framework which enables you to define the state of mind of your potential buyers. Specifically, you need to know how close they are to making a purchase. Sometimes, especially for problem buys, the bulk of your target audience can be a long way from making a purchase. They need a lot of information about the product and they want to think about it at length.

It is for this reason that the idea of moving potential customers gradually towards a purchase developed. You need to think in terms of moving your prospective buyers through a series of stages, which can be broadly grouped into the three following categories:

1 Knowing about a product.
2 Thinking about or evaluating a product.
3 Acting on a decision to buy or reject the product.

All new firms or firms entering new markets start from a position of total ignorance. Potential buyers do not know anything about the company or the products it offers. It is the task of the firm to gradually make customers aware of its existence, to educate them about the benefits of buying its products, to convince them that their products offer more than those of the competition, and to persuade them to place an order. Finally, unless you sell once in a lifetime purchases, you will want your customers to be satisfied so that they return to you next time they buy. If you achieve all these tasks you will have progressed from a position of ignorance to one of goodwill, as illustrated in fig. 11.1.

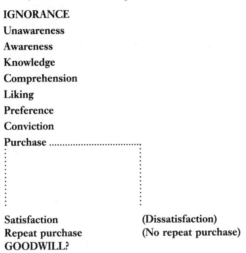

IGNORANCE

Unawareness

Awareness

Knowledge

Comprehension

Liking

Preference

Conviction

Purchase ....

Satisfaction　　　　　　　(Dissatisfaction)

Repeat purchase　　　　　(No repeat purchase)

GOODWILL?

Fig. 11.1 The ignorance – goodwill system

Although some of these stages do seem to be very similar they can be grouped together (into knowing, thinking, acting, for example) for the purpose of planning promotional campaigns. However, these fine gradations are often essential for analysing the company's position in the marketplace and for distinguishing and identifying areas in which problems arise.

Planning promotional campaigns

The need for a plan

How much money will you spend this year on marketing communications activities? Advertising, exhibitions, mailshots, perhaps a PR event or two, brochures and perhaps a few promotional freebies dished out to valued customers? These activities can cost a lot of money.

Consider now how you would approach spending the same amount of money on say, a new computer system. Before you even began to approach the task of buying the computer much deliberation would have taken place about the drawbacks of your current manual system. You would then have talked in general terms about the idea of computerizing, gradually identifying more and more tasks which the computer could perform. In this way a fairly detailed specification for the new computer system would have materialized: a set of criteria which must be achieved by potential suppliers of the system if they are to win your order and your cash. You then search the marketplace comparing suppliers, their products and the benefits offered to your company. You would evaluate these competitors with the aim of spending your money as wisely as possible. You want as much computer capacity as you can possibly buy for your money, and you want it to be appropriate to your company's needs. You may buy parts of the system from different suppliers. Once in operation you will evaluate all parts of the system. If you expand it or replace it in future you will not return to products or suppliers who have offered poor value for money the first time round.

How closely does your spending of marketing money follow this pattern? Consider a framework for the spending of marketing money based quite simply on the logical process followed by most buyers of a new computer system. In both cases you want to optimize your returns from spending your money.

Where are you now?

There are not many companies who would allocate money to the purchase of a new computer without a thorough analysis which enabled an informed decision to be taken. Why should the allocation of finance to marketing communications activities be any different? Assuming you have a good product or service it is ignorance which limits your sales – the ignorance of potential customers about your company and its products. Conversely, it is goodwill which increases sales. Your first step, for each target segment, is to define your company's position on the ignorance-goodwill scale objectively. Research has shown that buyers' information of suppliers is often very incomplete. Ignorance is far greater than suppliers usually think. Companies also have a natural tendency to exaggerate their prominence and standing in the marketplace. They underestimate ignorance and overestimate goodwill.

Unless you accept that you are right at the top of the scale, with ignorance reigning supreme, it is essential to carry out some kind of objective market research. You could carry out a small telephone survey, or some personal interviews, asking a few very simple questions to a small sample of potential buyers. Calls should be very brief and to the point, as shown in the following case study of Prince Components, a company producing components for several industries.

Prince Components
Telephone survey

To find out how potential buyers in the water industry viewed Prince Components and its products enabling it to establish its position on the ignorance – goodwill scale with that target audience, the company devised the following brief telephone questionnaire.

1 Can you tell me the names of any firms who supply
 XXXX components? YES/NO
 (*If Prince Components mentioned, go to 3*)

2 Have you heard of a firm called Prince Components?

YES/NO

(If NO, terminate)

3 Can you tell me some products Prince Components supply?
(If none, terminate. If complete list given, go to 5)

4 Did you know that Prince Components supply XXXX?

5 What would you say were the main reasons for doing business with Prince Components?

6 Are there any alternative suppliers that you prefer to do business with?

YES/NO

(If NO, go to 8)

7 If so why?

8 Have you ever bought from Prince Components?

YES/NO

(If NO go to 10)

9 Do you regard them as your regular supplier of these products?

YES/NO

10 Have you any intention, at the present time, to buy from Prince Components?

YES/NO

The answers to those questions would tell Prince Components at what point on the ignorance – goodwill scale they were failing with many potential buyers. For example, perhaps buyers didn't understand some of the benefits offered by the product. If so, this would be an area that would be particularly stressed in future promotional campaigns.

Where do you want to be in 12 months time?

Having defined your current position on the ignorance – goodwill scale you can now formulate your objectives in terms of improving on your position on that scale.

Prince Components
Promotional objectives

As a result of the telephone survey Prince Components realized that the company suffered from a very disappointing level of customer awareness and knowledge in the marketplace. Prince Components' promotional objectives would therefore be:

1 To make 80 per cent of potential buyers in the target market aware of the company and its range of products.

2 To make 40 per cent of the target market understand the benefits of buying from Prince Components.

3 To move 20 per cent of the target audience towards a state of preference for the product.

4 To make actual sales to 5 per cent of the target audience.

As shown in this example of Prince Components, promotional objectives should seek to move the target audience down the ignorance – goodwill scale. Of course, to move even a small percentage of the potential market to the goodwill end of the scale you will need to achieve success in the earlier steps of, for example, awareness and knowledge, with much larger numbers. Having clarified your promotional objectives, you need to devise a strategy capable of achieving them.

How shall you get there?

When buying that new computer there are really two stages between defining the specification and spending the money. The first step is an information search, comparing the benefits offered by different suppliers, the second step involves identifying the supplier whose package of benefits most closely matches your requirements. It is the same for marketing.

As far as marketing communications are concerned the two stages are: firstly comparing the benefits offered by different communications techniques; secondly identifying those techniques whose 'message sending' strengths most closely match your communications objectives. These topics lend themselves very well to discussion round the table by your marketing team. If you are going to match the strengths of each promotional technique to your own marketing communications objectives, you must be quite clear about the distinctive strengths of each communications tool. These strengths are summarized below.

Distinctive strengths of individual promotional techniques

Advertising
1 Mass communication of simple messages.
2 Increasing awareness.
3 Stimulating interest and enquiries.
4 Reaching unknown customers.
5 Reminding knowledgeable target audiences.

Direct mail
1 Targeting specific audiences.
2 Making impact.
3 Improving awareness and knowledge.
4 Stimulating responses.
5 Reminding existing customers.
6 Initiating relationships.

Public relations
1 Developing understanding and liking of a company and its products.
2 Sending complex messages.
3 Reaching the harder to get at corners of the audience, for example senior staff.
4 Enhancing relationships and goodwill.

Literature
1 Informing in depth, especially complex or technical details.
2 Increasing understanding through spelling out benefits.
3 Enabling the customer to make up his own mind.
4 Enhancing credibility or image.
5 Improving the presentation of the sales force.

Exhibitions
1 Improving understanding through demonstrating benefits.
2 Facilitating comparisons with competitors.
3 Making personal contacts.
4 Generating high quality sales leads.
5 Reaching unknown customers.

Sales promotion
1 Offering a short-term incentive to buy.
2 Attracting attention at point of sale.
3 Improving the impact of mailshots.

Telesales
1 Facilitating repeat ordering.
2 Reminding existing customers or prospects.
3 Qualifying leads.
4 Making appointments through cold calling or following up mailshots.

Personal selling
1 Building preference.
2 Handling objections.
3 Closing sales.
4 Fostering relationships with existing customers.
5 Maximizing repeat business.
6 Informing and reminding if audience numbers are very small and/or the conveyance of the information is particularly important.

It is important to stress that this list only represents a guideline as points of emphasis will vary according to different markets. For example, the strength of advertising and press releases will vary from one market to another depending on the authority of that market's trade journals. This underlines the importance of pooling the marketing experience within your firm (and that of external advisors) and generating an accurate and realistic list of media strengths. Of course everybody needs to experiment from time to time, but if you closely monitor the results of your promotional activities you will continually add to your own experience, helping you to make more informed decisions in the future.

PAFEC's TV campaign

Formed in 1976, PAFEC's sales of engineering software had risen to 17 million by 1987. For years it had promoted itself in the conventional way, using seminars, exhibitions, direct mail and advertisements in appropriate trade journals. However, PAFEC were not convinced that they were reaching a sufficiently wide target audience especially as the target audience was very large, and included organizations involved in architecture and mapping as well as engineering.

PAFEC therefore considered a wide range of alternative media including national press, technical press, inflight magazines, posters, TV and even London taxis. To evaluate these alternatives they came up with the following value for money formula:

$$\frac{\text{percentage of total population} \times \text{percentage of decision makers} \times \text{impact}}{\text{cost}}$$

The impact rating was subjective, and the cost rating was based on their estimate of what a campaign in each media category would cost to achieve similar coverage of the target audience. The following value for money table emerged:

Medium	Specifying engineers	All decision makers
Technical press	1.13	0.5
TV	0.47	0.47
National press	0.18	0.2
Posters	0.15	0.18
Taxis	0.08	—

As expected, the technical press proved to be the best way of reaching specialist engineers, but TV was almost as cost-effective at reaching general managers, and it would reach a lot more of them. PAFEC therefore took the brave decision to venture into TV advertising, but the risks were minimized by limiting the campaign initially to their local region, Central TV, which was estimated to cover 24 per cent of the country's manufacturing industry.

PAFEC was very careful in the scheduling of its ads, insisting on slots next to news, current affairs and business programmes. It also negotiated on price, securing a 30 per cent discount on rate card costs. The ad occupied two or three thirty second slots almost every day on Central ITV or Channel 4 for the whole of June. The cost of the campaign was £69,000 for air time and £20,000 for production costs. However, PAFEC recovered a total of £34,000 of these costs from two hardware manufacturers whose equipment featured in the ads, giving a net cost of £55,000 for the campaign.

The ad gave a freefone number for enquiries, and PAFEC manned the lines with its own staff. Respondents were sent a product brochure immediately and were later followed up by the telesales unit, with warm prospects receiving sales visits. The campaign generated 303 enquiries, including 182 (60 per cent) from the senior managers the campaign was directed at. Only 7.5 per cent of the respondents had heard of PAFEC before the campaign. Cost per qualified lead was high (£240), but some simple pre- and post- campaign research showed a huge increase in awareness of PAFEC and knowledge of its product. This improved company profile helped to increase the effectiveness of other promotional activities. For example, response rates to the company's seminar mailshots doubled. Less quantifiable feedback from customers and other contacts also convinced PAFEC that the campaign was very good value for money in terms of the awareness generated and the positive effects on the company's image.

A number of lessons can be learnt from the PAFEC campaign.

1 TV advertising is expensive – but not as expensive as many people think if you buy the time wisely and get some help with the costs, for example, through a joint venture with another company.

2 You need to pay very close attention to detail in all promotional campaigns. PAFEC specified exactly when the ads should be shown (despite having to pay more as a result), so that they went out at the best possible time to reach their target audience.

3 PAFEC is no longer a very small company, but it still has a limited budget, from which it wants to derive maximum value for money. It is that kind of planning which enabled PAFEC to optimize the returns on its limited promotional budget, and that kind of attitude which enabled the company to grow from a turnover of nothing to £17 million in ten years.

A promotional strategy planner

A useful framework to guide your discussions on promotional strategy is shown in fig. 11.2. This simple spreadsheet indicates the type of activity which is most relevant to your promotional objective for your target audience. From this you can get an idea of the structure and cost of your promotional effort for the year to come.

Promotional objectives	Advertising	Direct mail	Public relations	Exhibitions	Literature	Sales promotion	Telesales	Personal selling
1 Awareness and knowledge Make 80 per cent of potential buyers aware of our company and its range of products	●		●	●				
2 Comprehension Make 40 per cent of the target market understand the benefits of buying from us				●	●	●		
3 Liking and preference Move 20 per cent of target audience to a state of liking or preference		●				●	●	●
4 Conviction and purchase Make sales to 5 per cent of the target audience						●		●

Fig. 11.2 Promotional strategy planner

Are you on the right path?

Just as you will look very carefully at the workings of the new computer system after it is installed, it is vital to check continuously that your marketing communications campaign is on the right path. There are two important aspects of this activity: monitoring the response, and reacting to those responses.

1 **Monitoring the response.** Unless you are going to employ fairly sophisticated pre-campaign and post-campaign research techniques, recording the response is the only objective way of evaluating the success of your activities. Responses must be monitored continuously and accurately if a valid record is to be kept. Replies to adverts or editorials which are sent to you by the magazine concerned can be recorded as you receive them, as can contacts made through mailshots, exhibitions or other events. More difficult are telephone enquiries. It is vital to ascertain where the caller came across your company name. It might be from your latest advert, it may be word of mouth, or many other possibilities. You must ensure that you or your staff ask it, record the answer and file the record correctly.

To fully appreciate the results of your expenditure on promotion, a central record must be kept, manually or on computer. The system must record all responses to each promotional initiative together with any subsequent follow up, such as the sending of literature, a telephone follow up, sales calls, and, hopefully, the ultimate placing of an order by the prospect. A specimen control form is shown in fig. 11.3. If responses are accurately monitored it should enable you to work out exactly whether, for example, any particular mailshot had been cost-effective. With minor amendments to suit the nature of the activity it can be adapted to all other promotional techniques. If you link the system with your customer and prospect records (examples given in figs. 5.1 and 5.2) the control form enables you to identify which customers were a result of which promotional activity. This information is very important, because the quality of responses is often more important than the quantity. If you know that a lot of your good customers were a result of a particular promotional activity, you can confidently spend more money on that activity.

2 **Reacting to responses.** Once you have recorded your responses even more vital is to react to them. According to research, the average time lag between receiving a response and actually following it up is 30 days! This obviously does not convey a very good impression. If a supplier appears to have so little interest in obtaining an order, what hope might there be that he would fulfil it efficiently? So a rigid system for reacting to enquiries is essential. The ideal system would be:

1 An immediate phone call to qualify the lead (ascertain that the respondent is interested in doing business rather than just being an information collector – or a competitor!).

2 Company literature or further details put in the post immediately.

3 Identification of all qualified leads who would like to be visited by someone from your firm.

4 Qualified leads passed on daily to your sales rep, distributor (or whoever does the selling) so that an appointment can be made promptly. Even if a visit is not urgent, making the appointment is.

How will you know when you have arrived?

The final thing you must do is to analyse you promotional campaign.

DIRECT MAIL CONTROL FORM

Code ....

Mailshot ....

Date ....

Cost ....

Number sent ....

Cost per mailer ....

Responses ....

% response ....

Cost per response ....

Qualified leads ....

Cost per lead ....

Existing customers ....

New prospects ....

Cost per prospect ....

Appointments made ....

Cost per appointment ....

Sales closed ....

Cost per sale ....

Average number of visits

per sale ....

Prospects ....

Customers ....

Value of sales ....

Fig. 11.3 Specimen control form for promotional activities

There are two elements of this evaluation:

1 Did you achieve your communications objectives?
2 How efficient was your allocation of resources?

Quite simply, the first question is asking if you spent your money well, and the second question whether you could have spent it better.

1 Did you achieve your objectives? Unless you have clear and measurable objectives in the first place, it is never possible to know whether you have been successful. If you do have proper objectives, there are two ways of determining whether you have achieved them.

a Survey. Carry out a simple survey of the kind similar to the one used by Prince Components (page 186-7) before the start of your promotional campaign. File the results. After the campaign carry out a second survey, (with different respondents) asking identical questions. By comparing the results you will see whether you have moved the target audience as far down the ignorance–goodwill scale as you had intended.

b Evaluate responses. A second possibility would be to determine, ahead of the campaign, some sort of yardstick (perhaps based on the ignorance–goodwill scale) in terms of the level of response you are hoping to gain from your target audience as a result of each step of the campaign. For instance, your initial objective might be to gain customer awareness or interest, and for this set a figure of, say, 200 enquiries. Each respondent would then be sent further details through the post followed by a telephone call. For the company to move further down the ignorance–goodwill scale a predetermined number of people, say 100, should wish to take a further step towards purchase, such as agreeing to an appointment with one of your company's salespersons. Your final objective would be achieved if, say, 25 of your prospects buy your product, so becoming new customers.

Predetermining these step by step objectives enables the firm to measure its success at all stages of the promotional campaign in a tangible way.

Neither of these methods is expensive. Both take time, but if you want your marketing to succeed you have to be prepared to invest time in managing it properly.

2 How efficiently was the budget spent? The second question is of even greater value for future decision making and the ability to answer it will depend entirely on an efficient system for recording responses. The example of Naylor Clayware in the last chapter showed how the company ran a successful campaign based on a free prize draw, meeting its targets for new customers, and increased sales. However, as a result of recording the responses it was possible to see that some aspects of the campaign were much more successful than others. Direct mail, for example, proved to be much more cost-effective than advertising. Accurate recording of responses enabled that firm to make better decisions for the following campaign. We also saw in Chapter 5 how the Polurrian Hotel improved its conversion rate of enquiries to bookings from 1 in 20 to 1 in 6 as a result of a carefully planned promotional strategy. However, it was only through the

keeping of an accurate control system that the hotel's owners could be certain of the cost-effectiveness of their high promotional expenditure.

Checklist: Effective promotional planning

1 Your approach to the spending of marketing money must be as careful and well planned as your approach to (seemingly) more major purchases, such as a new computer. In fact, during the course of a year you will often spend more money on marketing activities than you would on a major purchase.

2 To plan effectively you must be aware of your current position. This should be defined using the ignorance – goodwill scale which will indicate to you how close the bulk of your potential customers are to actually making a purchase from your company.

3 The objective of your promotional spending must be to move customers further along this scale.

4 Having defined your objectives the most crucial planning decision is determining which promotional techniques are most capable of achieving objectives. Only spend money on suitable activities.

5 Once your campaign is underway you must have a system which allows you to monitor the results so that you can evaluate your results properly. Evaluating this year's results will help you to get more value for money out of next year's spending.

6 More important than anything else is a swift response to people who make enquiries as a result of your promotion.

Planning specific promotional activities

Having planned your campaign you will need to get down to the nitty-gritty of putting into practice the specific promotional techniques that you have chosen to use. As explained in Chapter 10, many promotional activities require lengthy advance planning. All require meticulous attention to detail. The only way to ensure that you perform on time all the little tasks that lead up to a successful exhibition or mailshot is to have a thorough plan, which lists all the jobs, however small, specifies deadlines and assigns responsibility to individuals for the satisfactory completion of each task. A spreadsheet or wallchart provides a good basis for such a planner. The example given in Chapter 6 (fig. 6.6) forms the ideal basis for such a chart.

To get the timing correct, you need to work back from your major deadline (such as the date of the exhibition you are planning for) and ask yourself: 'what do I have to do by when?' For example, you would need your literature for the exhibition one month before the event to allow time for any problems, such as errors made by the printer, to be rectified. The printer may require artwork and photographs one month before that, which will mean booking a photography session three to four weeks earlier. The products to be photographed will have to be made before that, which probably means that you are already at about four months before the date of the event itself. However, if you do not plan, in detail, well ahead, you will, at best, have some very unpleasant panics. At worst you will mount some very unprofessional campaigns which could damage rather than enhance your image.

Summary

1 Due to the difficulty of communicating with a remote audience, firms should not try to rush the process that leads to a sale. They should plan a phased promotional strategy which moves the target audience through the ignorance – goodwill scale in a series of steps.

2 The planning of a promotional campaign should be given as much management time and attention as, for example, the purchase of new capital equipment. The chief management task is to select the promotional techniques which are most appropriate to the achievement of the firm's communications objectives.

3 Once a promotional strategy has been devised, it should be implemented thoroughly and monitored carefully. Meticulous attention to detail is essential if the many tasks which make up a promotional campaign are to be coordinated successfully.

Action

For each market segment in which your firm operates, answer the following questions.

1 How many potential customers are there in the market segment? If it is an organizational market, how many individuals influence decision making and therefore should receive promotional messages from your company?

2 On average, across your market segment, what is your approximate position on the ignorance – goodwill scale?

3 Formulate three specific communications objectives that will enable you to move your target audience down the ignorance – goodwill scale.

4 Using the promotional strategy planner (fig. 11.2), work out the most effective allocation of your promotional resources to achieve the communications objectives you have set.

5 How will you know whether you have achieved your objectives? Will you carry out pre- and post- campaign marketing research? If not, what other yardsticks will you set to judge your performance?

6 What system do you have for recording the responses to your promotional activity?

7 Who is responsible for ensuring that your firm reacts appropriately and efficiently to enquiries and responses?

Index